ROUTLEDGE LIBRARY EDITIONS: ETHICS

Volume 21

COMMON-SENSE ETHICS

COMMON-SENSE ETHICS

C. E. M. JOAD

Routledge
Taylor & Francis Group

LONDON AND NEW YORK

First published in 1921 by Methuen & Co Ltd

This edition first published in 2021
by Routledge
2 Park Square, Milton Park, Abingdon, Oxon OX14 4RN

and by Routledge
52 Vanderbilt Avenue, New York, NY 10017

Routledge is an imprint of the Taylor & Francis Group, an informa business

© 1921 C. E. M. Joad

All rights reserved. No part of this book may be reprinted or reproduced or utilised in any form or by any electronic, mechanical, or other means, now known or hereafter invented, including photocopying and recording, or in any information storage or retrieval system, without permission in writing from the publishers.

Trademark notice: Product or corporate names may be trademarks or registered trademarks, and are used only for identification and explanation without intent to infringe.

British Library Cataloguing in Publication Data
A catalogue record for this book is available from the British Library

ISBN: 978-0-367-85624-3 (Set)
ISBN: 978-1-00-305260-9 (Set) (ebk)
ISBN: 978-0-367-47050-0 (Volume 21) (hbk)
ISBN: 978-1-00-303306-6 (Volume 21) (ebk)

Publisher's Note
The publisher has gone to great lengths to ensure the quality of this reprint but points out that some imperfections in the original copies may be apparent.

Disclaimer
The publisher has made every effort to trace copyright holders and would welcome correspondence from those they have been unable to trace.

COMMON-SENSE ETHICS

BY
C. E. M. JOAD

WITH A PREFACE BY
PROFESSOR A. H. WILDON CARR

METHUEN & CO. LTD.
36 ESSEX STREET W.C
LONDON

First Published in 1921

PREFACE

By H. WILDON CARR

THERE is no class of judgments to which we appeal with more absolute confidence in the ultimate unanimity of different minds than moral judgments. If men have been found to defend the Holy Inquisition, the Roman gladiatorial shows, negro slavery, or frightfulness in war, it is not because they differ from their fellows in their judgments concerning what constitutes right and wrong, but because they can make appeal to a sentiment in human nature which is not the subject of dispute but the arbiter. When we try, however, to give definite form and substance to this sentiment itself,—and this is the aim of the philosophical science of Ethics,—we find serious difficulty. It was manifested in wide divergency in the ancient ethical theories, and it is a problem dividing different schools of thought in philosophy to-day. Moreover, it is a problem to which no one is really indifferent, for it involves the problem of problems,—the nature and meaning of life.

This book is a study, an earnest, fresh and living study of the ethical problem by a young philosopher who has reflected deeply on the metaphysical theories of the ancient and modern periods and has tried seriously to bring them into accord and to discover in them some guidance, particularly in regard to the political and social evolution which the present generation is witnessing. He describes his own view as that of common-sense Ethics. But by common sense it is clear that he does not intend to class himself with unphilosophical opinion, either in reasoned or contemptuous opposition to philosophical theory.

A generation ago it was very widely held by writers on

Ethics that the ethical problem, so far as the principle by which conduct should be ruled is concerned, depended on a previous question and was governed by the decision in answer to it: " Is life worth living ? " It was taken for granted that if on inquiry this question has to be answered in the negative, then all conduct which makes *effectually* for the extinction of life is good conduct, and all that makes *effectually* for the furtherance of life is bad. And this seemed in fact to distinguish not merely individual ethical systems, but to mark a fundamental divergence of orientation between different systems of philosophy and also between different religions. Broadly it marked the profound difference between East and West which Schopenhauer was the first to discover and make familiar to us. We have now come to see that life is an activity, or force, or reality, which cannot in any way be affected by our individual opinion in regard to its desirability, measured by any possible or impossible hedonistic calculus. A consensus of modern research, scientific and philosophic, biological and psychological, has antiquated all the ethical and religious theories which made life subservient to a force and purpose superior to it and independent of it. The will to live is the nature of life, something in the very fact and expression of life, and not a power, rational or irrational, which raises us above life and enables us to control it. To appreciate the significance of this in individual, social and political action seems to me the underlying motive of the author in this book.

There are two movements in quite recent scientific research which seem to have had a considerable influence on the author in the formation of his theory. Both are mentioned, and their importance referred to, although no detailed exposition of them is given in the book. They are first the Behaviourist theory and second the psychoanalytic psychology and psychotherapy of Freud and Jung. The Behaviourist theory and method has been adopted and brought into prominence by some of the leading psychologists of America. The form and practical application of the theory is new, but in effect it is the revival of an old, almost venerable, theory—the old theory of Descartes of the *bête-machine*. It declares that there is no entity,—consciousness or thought,—constituting a special class of existences, requiring a particular method of their own,—introspection,—in order to bring them within mental apprehension.

The Psycho-analytic theory is in a certain aspect the direct antithesis of the Behaviourist theory and method, for the responses we observe in animal behaviour are according to the psycho-analysts never to be taken at their face value. This is always illusive and though unconscious purposely deceptive. Behaviour has to be interpreted, and the interpretation rests on the concept of a reality which is unconscious, yet essentially active and mental. In another aspect, however, the theory may be said to agree with Behaviourism, namely in its thoroughgoing mechanism and determinism. To me, indeed, the difference is more striking than the resemblance, for while behaviourism seems to triumph only when and in so far as it succeeds in explaining psychical phenomena by rejecting psychology, the Psycho-analytic theory has a psychological explanation of every fact of experience. The only point in which they may be said to agree is in the fact that each in its way gives a negative answer to William James's now famous question, "Does consciousness exist?"

These then seem to me to be the moulding influences under which Mr. Joad has worked out his theory of a life force manifesting itself as unconscious impulse, for which it should be the main purpose of æsthetical, social and political activity to discover the most perfect expression. His book falls naturally into two parts, and we are told in the introduction that we may skip the first part if we are not philosophically inclined. This is not my advice. The exposition of the Utilitarian and Intuitionist theories, and the account of Plato's theory, and the criticism upon them, are a necessary introduction to the view which the author terms common-sense Ethics.

H. WILDON CARR

CONTENTS

CHAP.		PAGE
	INTRODUCTION	xi

PART I

PHILOSOPHICAL OR TRADITIONAL ETHICS

I	UTILITARIANISM AND THE PHILOSOPHY OF PLEASURE	1
II	INTUITIONISM AND THE MORAL SENSE	21
III	THE FORM OF THE GOOD	65
IV	SUMMARY OF ETHICAL THEORIES AND THEIR RESULTS	78

PART II

EMPIRICAL OR COMMON-SENSE ETHICS

V	THE PSYCHOLOGY OF IMPULSE	95
VI	THE PLACE OF IMPULSE IN POLITICS AND SOCIETY	131
VII	IMPULSE AS THE EXPRESSION OF THE LIFE FORCE	176
	INDEX	205

INTRODUCTION

THE following chapters purport to constitute a book on Ethics. Whether those who read them will agree that they have anything to do with Ethics at all is doubtful. The possibility of this doubt arises from a very real disagreement as to what the study of Ethics is about. Most philosophical controversies when analyzed are found to be controversies about what exactly it is that is the subject of the controversy, and controversies about Ethics are no exception to this rule. There is in fact a complete lack of agreement as to the subject matter, the scope, the method, and the object of Ethics.

Nor are the philosophers entirely to blame.

It contributes to the confusion that Ethics is a pursuit in which everybody is an expert. Whereas it is held that a man needs special training and experience before he may presume to speak with authority on architecture, painting, engineering or chemistry, most men believe themselves to know the difference between good and evil by the light of nature. Elderly relatives in particular are an inexhaustible fount of moral maxim. The mother is thought fully qualified to instruct her child on the meaning of naughtiness, the priest his congregation on the path to perdition, and the fact that where the object of both is to deter from wrongdoing, the one means inconvenience to herself, and the other disobedience to a written word, believed to be divinely inspired, only serves to show that usage can be made to countenance any meaning of morality or immorality that happens to be convenient at the moment. Ethics in short is every one's preserve; it is like a hat which has lost its shape because everybody wears it.

Contemplating the welter of material thus presented, philosophers have endeavoured to work it up into a clearly defined branch of knowledge like biology or physics. The attempt has not been very successful. What has happened is that philosophers have become interested in different classes of ethical questions, and, by a natural process of reasoning, have insisted that the particular questions in which they were interested and which formed the topics of their books, were the proper subject matter of Ethics.

Thus a number of quite different problems have each been regarded as the central problem of Ethics, which has been variously defined as the attempt—

(1) To discover the good.
(2) To find a meaning for the words right and wrong.
(3) To find a criterion by which to distinguish right from wrong.
(4) To describe the nature of the moral sense.
(5) To lay down rules for moral conduct.

With regard to each of these inquiries sufficiently intelligible results can be and have been reached. Why then yet another book about Ethics?

The answer to this question is to be found in a conviction on the part of the writer that Ethics really ought to have something to do with life. Ethics ought to tell you how to be good or happy, that is, if you want to be; or why it is impossible to be either good or happy; or why, though it is possible to be both good and happy, it is not possible to tell you how to be either. In short the writer takes the view that the conclusions of Ethics ought to have some relation to the business of living.

Now it is, I think, a fact that the conclusions arrived at by philosophical ethical theorists do not have this relation. I do not believe that a knowledge of all the philosophical ethical theories in the world would in any way assist a man in the business of living: if life is a duty, they would not help him to be good; if it is an art, they would not confer mastery in its technique.

Many people who reason about Ethics for the first time are convinced at an early stage by the specious arguments of those who hold that pleasure is the only good, and the only possible object of human desire. I remember with what excitement I was myself converted to this view, and set about life in a new spirit, believing that I had knocked the bottom out of virtue, and need not bother myself any more about being unselfish; for was not all unselfishness just a somewhat peculiar method of getting pleasure? It was something of a shock to find that my new convictions did not in practice make the slightest difference. I went on acting in precisely the same way as before, and was not noticeably worse in point of conduct than I had been in the days when I still thought there was some virtue in being good.

Nor was mine an exceptional case. There is absolutely no evidence either to show that the average moral philosopher is in any way better or worse than men who have never heard of John Stuart Mill, or that the followers of John Stuart Mill are in any way better or worse than their mortal enemies of the moral sense school. There is, on the contrary, plenty of evidence that the moral philosopher is just as liable as his wife to lose his temper when he misses a train or breaks his bootlace; that ethical philosophers like Bentham and Aristippus, who propounded theories of such outrageous immorality that no roué has yet been discovered with the capacity to live up to them, were men of pre-eminently blameless conduct, who recognized in every act of their lives the moral sanctions they denied in theory; and that being a philosopher in the technical sense of the word has nothing to do with possessing a philosophic outlook on life in general. The philosopher, in the commonly accepted sense of the word, is a man who maintains an attitude of serene equanimity in face alike of the inevitable toothaches and pimples of experience, and of such tragedies as life has to offer; the expert on philosophical Ethics can refute the arguments of the pleasure philosophers and knows what the neo-Platonists thought about the good. The first is a master of the art of life; the second of the theories of philosophers: but the knowledge of the one does not help him to attain the serenity of the other. In so far as ethical theories have had any practical effect whatever, it has been of an inhibitory rather than an inspiring character. Instead of revealing a vision of what life might be, they have denounced it for what it is. People have found in ethical systems a convenient clothes-line for airing their own moral prejudices; moral codes have tended to become a catalogue of "Don't's," and writers on conscience have succeeded in taking the sugar out of our tea without preventing our drinking it.

This failure on the part of Ethics to apply to the actual problems of life is, I think, the inevitable result of the methods by which Ethics has been pursued—the methods of *a priori* reasoning. Certain general principles, the truth of which is supposed to be immediately perceived, are used as the starting point of an inquiry which proceeds by the methods of logical reasoning to construct an elaborate system on the basis thus provided. The result may be logical and consistent : if the reasoning is good it is bound to be ; but it has no necessary relation to life. The statements made in the course of the inquiry are statements not about life, but about the philosopher's reasoning about life : the results achieved are a reflection not of the world, but of the philosopher's mind.

It is too commonly assumed that the laws by which mind works must necessarily produce results which are true of life, and that conclusions which are satisfying to mind must necessarily apply to something. The remoteness of the conclusions of ethical systems from the facts of human life shows that a process of logical reasoning, satisfactory as its conclusions may be in the realm of mathematics, is not in itself an adequate method for the treatment of life.

Life, unlike mathematics, is various and changing. It persistently eludes the attempt of mind to gather it up under a few comprehensive formulæ. It is tentative, provisional and inconclusive, and for this very reason refuses to accommodate itself to the demands which philosophic systems have made of it.

Thus it is in part their very completeness and definitiveness which make the systems of philosophic Ethics inapplicable to life. They have laid it down that the good is X, and the meaning of right is Y, when the individual finds in practice that the good is X to-day and Z to-morrow, while as for the meaning of right and wrong, it changes continually according to his mood and his feelings towards the person who happens to be right or wrong at the moment. Life is like a play in which the individual has to learn his part while he is speaking it. Philosophical systems assume him word perfect from the beginning.

It is suggested therefore that a book on Ethics which is to

apply to life, can neither evolve a system nor establish a standard. It will not begin with general principles and proceed by deduction from them, starting that it is along a road indicated by mind in the hope that it will somehow lead in the end to life. It will start rather with the observation of life, and be glad if the results fall into any kind of order, or admit of any kind of generalization.

And these generalizations will be neither final nor infallible, for they will be conditioned by the changing and elusive character of the subject matter about which they generalize. Perhaps in generalizing at all about Ethics and psychology, we are going beyond our evidence ; perhaps the individual's desires and inhibitions are too personal and idiosyncratic to be ranked in common with those of others under any formula : perhaps it is the power or generalization which gives us our chief superiority in mistake over the animals. But since thinking is little more than a process of stringing together likely generalizations, and since, in spite of all the evidence to the contrary, men including writers do think, readers must be asked to put up with the generalizing habit, provided that writers do not try to pass off their generalizations as absolute and infallible truths.

Given the twofold object, first of demonstrating the irrelevance for the actual problems of life of philosophical Ethics, and secondly of indicating a method likely to yield more practical results, the following book falls naturally into two parts.

It will be the object of the first part to give a brief survey of the leading theories of philosophical Ethics. It will indicate the conclusions that they reach, and will attempt, in the spirit of the theories with which it deals, to achieve a logical reconciliation of their differences. I have tried to avoid all technical language in dealing with these theories, and to present them briefly and clearly. But the treatment is here primarily philosophical, and if the reader dislikes philosophy, he is recommended to begin at Part II.

The second part leaves the region of traditional philosophy and enters the realm of psychology and politics. Beginning with the individual, it asks what most men do as a fact desire, and then proceeds to consider in what way their desires can be realized. The method of treatment changes with the change of subject matter ; it is discursive rather than philosophical and ranges from psycho-analysis to Guild Socialism. We leave the region of truths which are true for all men in all ages (truths, that is, that apply to no men who have ever lived), and consider the typical modern man in the typical modern community.

It is hoped that this part will be found to make up in verve what it lacks in logic, and to compensate by an increased vitality of treatment for its philosophically impressionist methods and provisional generalizations.

C. E. M. J.

COMMON-SENSE ETHICS

PART I

PHILOSOPHICAL OR TRADITIONAL ETHICS

CHAPTER I

UTILITARIANISM AND THE PHILOSOPHY OF PLEASURE

§ 1. What the Utilitarians Believed

I PROPOSE in this and the two following chapters to describe and to discuss some of the main theories about Ethics that have been propounded by philosophers.

In this chapter I shall deal with the group of theories which hold, in the first place, that actions are to be judged as right or wrong according to their consequences; and in the second, that in assessing those consequences pleasure or happiness is the only thing which can properly be regarded as valuable. It is clear that the second proposition, namely that pleasure is the only thing of value, does not necessarily follow from the first, namely that the rightness or wrongness of actions depends on their consequences, and that it is possible for the one proposition to be true although the other is untrue. Philosophers who have held the first position have, however, as a general rule subscribed to the second, and it will therefore be convenient to consider them together.

The theories in question have been very popular among ethical writers, from the early Greek thinkers down to our own day. John Stuart Mill may, however, be regarded as perhaps the most typical exponent of this school of thought, and I propose therefore to examine the theories chiefly in the form in which they were propounded by him. He called his doctrine Utilitarianism, or the Theory of Utility, and he states it as follows : " Actions are right in proportion as they tend to promote happiness, wrong as they tend to produce the reverse of happiness. By happiness is intended pleasure and the absence of pain ; by unhappiness, pain and the privation of pleasure." " Pleasure and freedom from pain are the only things desirable as ends." When we ask the question, whose happiness and whose pain are meant, the answer is the happiness and pain of the greatest number.

In this connection Mill refers us to Bentham's famous maxim, to the effect that " Everybody should count as one, and nobody as more than one."

Those actions therefore are " right " or " ought " to be performed which produce the best consequences, and the best consequences are the greatest happiness of the greatest number.

In addition to the above doctrine, Mill adopted a peculiar psychological view with regard to the nature of pleasure. Not only does he hold as a matter of ethics that pleasure *ought* to be pursued, but as a matter of psychology he holds that nothing but pleasure can be desired, and that nothing but pleasure *can* therefore be pursued.

When pressed for a proof of this theory, he points out quite rightly that questions of ultimate ends are incapable of proof in the ordinary sense of the word, for whatever can be proved to be good can only be so proved by being shown to be a means to something which is recognized as good without proof. " The medical art is proved to be good by its conducing to health ; but how is it possible to prove that health is good ? " The only way therefore in which we can show something ultimate to be good, is by looking into our consciousness and seeing whether we really think it so. When desiring to prove his theory that pleasure is the only good, Mill has recourse therefore to the methods of practised self-consciousness and self-observation.

These methods lead him to the following conclusion :

" Desiring a thing and finding it pleasant, aversion to it and thinking of it as painful, are phenomena entirely inseparable, two different modes of naming the same psychological fact: to think of an object as desirable . . . and to think of it as pleasant are one and the same thing : and to desire anything except in proportion as the idea of it is pleasant is a physical and metaphysical impossibility."

These quotations are sufficient to give a brief summary of the Utilitarian doctrine. It will be seen that it divides itself into two distinct parts : (1) That the rightness and wrongness of actions must be judged by their consequences, and (2) that of these consequences, pleasure alone is good and pleasure alone ought to be promoted.

In this chapter I propose only to consider the second of these tenets, namely that pleasure alone is good, and to assume that the first is correct. Consideration will be given to the first position, namely that actions must be judged and assessed by their consequences and only by their consequences in the second chapter, in which I propose to discuss Intuitionist theories.

The view that pleasure is the only good is held in two distinct forms. (*A*) That as a matter of psychological fact only pleasure can be desired. (*B*) That other things can in point of fact be desired, but only pleasure ought to be desired.

§ 2. Pleasure as the Sole Object of Desire

(*A*) The first of these views, which is usually called hedonism from the Greek word ἡδονή (pleasure), is as old as the Greeks if not older. It was the doctrine of the Cyrenaic school of Greek Philosophy, and was expounded with great force of dialectic by a philosopher called Aristippus. It has a disarming and specious simplicity which attaches to all extreme theories, and may be propounded with overwhelming effect by young libertines and revolutionaries anxious to discredit the canons of orthodox morality for their own purposes. The plausibility of the theory in fact renders it particularly attractive to those who have reflected for the first time upon ethics, and it is always a little disappointing to find, on deeper reflection, that truth really is not as simple as all that. The theory derives this plausibility from the fact that there is no class of actions which cannot be shown by very good arguments to have been performed with the object of producing pleasure for the doer, and solely with that object.

Let us consider an instance of an apparently unselfish action performed from so-called altruistic motives. A has ten shillings at Christmas and spends it on presents for himself, whereas B, also having ten shillings, spends it on presents for his little brothers and sisters; it might appear at first sight that whereas A was being selfish and acting only for his own pleasure, B was being unselfish and acting for the pleasure of others.

"Not a bit of it," says the hedonist! "B's action exemplifies my theory as much as A's, for B is aiming at his own pleasure just as much as A, only B happens to get his pleasure in a different way. Whereas A obtains most pleasure from things which indulge his appetites and satisfy his acquisitive desires, B obtains it by indulging his impulses towards generosity which secure for him the approbation of his conscience and the gratitude of his brothers and sisters to boot. People like B are so constituted that they get most pleasure by giving pleasure to other people. Thus they choose to indulge their tendencies to self-denial and their instincts of generosity. The result is that they benefit their fellows, who naturally call them unselfish, whereas they call people like A selfish; but this does not mean that the B's are not thorough-going hedonists all the same, and aiming all the time at the pleasure which pleases them, just as their opposites secure by more direct means the pleasure to which they are attracted. Similarly it may be shown that any course of action, such as voluntary martyrdom at the stake, is undertaken solely because the agent thinks that by its means he will secure the maximum of pleasure in the long run: otherwise of course he would not act in that way."

Any virtue may be completely shown up by these methods. Temperance is simply the exercise of our faculties in such a way as to combine the maximum of pleasure with the minimum of pain: Charity is a proposal by A that B should relieve C: Patriotism is a love of country, other people's preferred: the only sin is to get found out and so on.

This theory is not only plausible but it is logically irrefutable. It is not possible to prove that people's actions are not dictated solely by the desire to secure pleasure for themselves. On the other hand there is not the least reason to suppose it to be true.

The best means of disproving it is to look into one's own consciousness and to find out whether one is in fact actuated by desire for pleasure, either present pleasure or pleasure in the long run in every action one undertakes. Does the theory, in short, square with the facts of consciousness?

When a man rushes into the street to save a child from falling under the wheels of a passing motor-car at the risk of his own life, does he stop to calculate that by doing so he will obtain more pleasure than by staying where he is, or does he act from an unthinking impulse to save the child's life? To me at least it is clear that he acts from impulse only. Many actions are purely impulsive, in the sense that the agent has no thought of any ulterior end to be gained by the action. Such actions are the result of the prompting of impulse, and no calculation on the part of mind influences the performance of the action. Acts of passion and anger are of this character. The man who beats his wife does not do so because he calculates that he will get the most pleasure by doing so, but because he is annoyed with his wife and wishes to vent his annoyance by beating her. This does not mean that he may not get pleasure by beating his wife; he probably will, the satisfaction of any impulse being a source of pleasure; but it does mean that the desire for pleasure was not the motive of the act.

Two distinct truths do in point of fact lie at the basis of the hedonist philosophy. It is true in the first place that the satisfaction of every impulse or desire is attended by pleasure. It is true in the second place that nothing can be regarded as ethically valuable in practice, except with reference to its effect upon human consciousness. Thus if an exhibition of unselfishness could be imagined to take place in a world devoid of conscious beings, such an exhibition, just because it would have no reference to any form of consciousness, would from the practical point of view be of no value. It would not help anybody to be good, nor would anybody feel it to be good.[1]

[1] For the intrinsic as opposed to the practical value of non-apprehended goodness see Chapter III, page 79.

These truths, the truth that satisfaction of desire brings pleasure, and the truth that the practical value of actions is to be sought ultimately in their effect upon some human consciousness, have been distorted into the theory that the pursuit of pleasure is the end of all our actions.

But to say that, because only consciousness is practically valuable, and because all satisfaction of desire brings pleasure to consciousness, it follows that the desire for pleasure is the mainspring of all our actions, is to put the cart before the horse.

What happens as a matter of psychology is that we desire specific things, and we obey specific impulses without actually thinking about pleasure or the chances of getting it one way or the other. Pleasure comes and clothes our mental state when we have acquired the thing, or satisfied the impulse, but that does not mean that the pleasure which came later was the motive which inspired our action to begin with.

The theory in fact becomes ludicrous when applied to primitive and impulsive actions, such as the blows a man strikes in anger, the inevitable flinching of countenance when a man shakes his fist under your nose, or the turning aside of the face to avoid a rapidly flying hockey ball. In all these cases we act purely impulsively without reflection.

To take an instance given by Canon Rashdall. "If the hedonistic psychology were true, every one must have been starved in early infancy. A young animal could not survive without sucking, and it would never on this theory have begun to suck, unless it had some reason to suppose that sucking would be a source of pleasure. Such knowledge it could only obtain from experience, and such experience it could not possibly possess a few hours after its birth."

It is clear that the first act of sucking is the result of an impulse of which absolutely no account can be given except the statement that it exists, and although the infant may suck at a later stage because it finds by experience that sucking produces pleasure, it is obvious that it did not suck with that motive to begin with.

Pleasure, then, though it may be attendant upon the satisfaction of every desire, is not the object of absolutely every desire, and some actions could never have been performed at all if pleasure was in fact the only possible object of desire.

So far is the hedonistic view from being the true one that we may notice as a matter of psychological interest, that desire for pleasure as opposed to desire for specific things is the most unsatisfactory form of desire, inasmuch as it constantly fails to attain its object, pleasure if pursued directly having a curious habit of eluding the pursuer. Thus entertainments which we attend because we desire pleasure, nourishing, in spite of all the evidence to the contrary, an invincible belief that they will produce it for us, are notoriously incapable of providing either intense or lasting pleasure.

That life would be tolerable but for its amusements, is a despairing commentary upon the Nemesis that appears to overtake the majority of our efforts to capture pleasure, by attending amusements and other functions which purport to supply it.

Pleasure, like beauty, cannot be taken by storm. It may not be pursued directly, but comes indirectly to invest our consciousness only when we have been actively engaged in pursuing and achieving something else. In particular it is wont to manifest itself when our faculties are fully developed, and are called into the fullest activity of which they are capable. This is the gist of Aristotle's famous account of pleasure in the tenth book of the Ethics, as of a something added when the activity of the best faculty is directed upon the best and most complete object. Aristotle takes a parallel from the case of health. When a healthy young man is engaged in activity calling forth his fullest powers, there is a superadded completion or perfection upon his health like a bloom. Now pleasure is of this character ; it comes as a superadded perfection, like the bloom upon the cheek of a young man, which, though not directly aimed at, may be taken as a sign that the powers of the mind and body are in an active and healthy state, that in other words the human machine is working smoothly.

For this reason paradoxically enough the most real and lasting pleasures have probably been found to arise in connection with work. The pleasures of that work which makes the heaviest demand upon our faculties, the pleasures of the athlete, the artist, the critic or the composer, the pleasures, in brief, of creative work are probably the most real pleasures known to mankind.

On these lines also is to be found an explanation of the element of uncertainty that attaches to pleasure. There is no certain recipe for the production of pleasure, just as there is no certain recipe for the production of beauty. The mathematician who multiplies seven by seven knows that the result will always and infallibly be forty-nine. The scientist knows that if hydrogen and oxygen are combined in certain proportions the result will infallibly be water. But the ingredients that will infallibly produce pleasure are unknown. Just because it eludes us if we desire it directly, just because it comes and clothes as it were absent-mindedly without purpose or design, a mental state which has been ardently concerned with the achievement of something else, there is always an element of chance or fluke about its manifestation.

It may indeed be probable that if the methods of its production were certainly known, if in fact it could be produced at will, it would cease to be pleasure and would become something different : for the pleasantness of pleasure seems to lie more than anything else in the unexpected quality that characterizes it. It is this element of chance in pleasure that makes it impossible for us to predict of experiences in life whether they will be valuable or not.

We have seen reasons above for doubting whether pleasure is, as the hedonists assert, the only possible object of human desire. It seems probable that besides actions which are dictated purely by impulse, with regard to which no desire of any kind is entertained or commonly put before himself by the agent, human beings can desire for their own sake a number of different things such as music, knowledge and beauty. By the term " desire for its own sake " I understand a desire which does not pursue its object as a means, a means namely for the production of pleasure to the person entertaining the desire ; a desire, that is, which does not connect the object desired with pleasure, or envisage the pleasure which its possession may produce. What these objects are which can be desired for their own sake, and which possess value in their own right, will be considered in the next chapter,

It is nevertheless possible, if not probable, that no whole can be regarded as valuable unless it possess some admixture of pleasure. It has been said above that in practice the only thing which is ultimately valuable from the point of view of ethics is some form of human consciousness. In a world of machines there would be for practical purposes no good or bad, no right or wrong. Mental states are the source and origin of practical ethical value, and also the test or arbiter by which the value of actions is to be judged. Now what seems to be possible if not probable with regard to pleasure, is that no mental state considered as a whole can be valuable unless it possesses an admixture of pleasure. We have noted above how pleasure tends to invest the mental state of the man who achieves a desired object, or exercises his faculties to the full : we may go further and assert that unless it does so, that mental state has no value.

We are committed therefore to the position that although when a man goes to a concert he desires music and not pleasure, nevertheless unless pleasure is an element attendant upon his appreciation of the music, the whole mental state that results from hearing the music is a state without value. This does not mean, however, that the whole mental state is valuable only in proportion to the amount of pleasure it contains. Such a statement would be tantamount to the assertion which we have already repudiated, that only pleasure is valuable, whereas the satisfaction of the desire for music has value on its own account apart from the pleasure which attends it, provided always that pleasure does attend it. The fact that the pleasure is superadded, gives the appreciation of the music a value in its own right, which it did not possess until the pleasure were superadded.

This is an apparent contradiction in algebra, which may yet hold true in psychology. It is a contradiction in algebra because it involves our saying that if x is a whole containing two elements y and z, and if y stands for the element of pleasure, and z for the other elements of value in the whole x, then (1) the value of x is 0, if the value of y is 0 ; yet (2) z has value in its own right apart from the value of y. Hence arises the paradoxical conclusion that the value of the part z plus the value of the part y is greater than the value of the whole x.

I have used this algebraic illustration simply to elucidate the point at issue, and not because I think that the circumstance that ethical reasoning leads to algebraical paradox is in any way to the discredit of ethical reasoning. Moreover, any one who thinks that it tends to obscure instead of to clarify the issue is at perfect liberty to leave it out.

As a result of this section therefore we may assert the following propositions:

(1) Pleasure is not the only thing which it is possible for human beings to desire.
(2) Other things may not only be desired besides pleasure, but may possess intrinsic value in their own right.
(3) No mental whole is valuable unless it contains a certain admixture of pleasure.

§ 3. Desire for Pleasure as a Duty

(B) If we hold the first of the two positions with regard to pleasure referred to above, namely that as a matter of psychological fact only pleasure can be desired, consideration of the truth of the second position, namely that pleasure and only pleasure ought to be desired, does not arise. There is no meaning in saying that we ought to desire pleasure, if we are so constituted psychologically that we can desire nothing else.

But it is possible to maintain that, although as a matter of psychology we do desire other things besides pleasure, only pleasure ought to be desired, pleasure being the only kind of good. This latter position was held by the philosopher Henry Sidgwick. It was also held implicitly by John Stuart Mill, the philosopher whom we are considering as a typical example of the Utilitarian school, however much he may have explicitly repudiated this particular doctrine in his writings. Explicitly Mill agreed with Jeremy Bentham, from whom he inherited his Utilitarian views, that only pleasure could in point of fact be desired. Mill, however, though the author of a work on logic, was more remarkable for philosophical insight than for logical consistency, and he frequently commits himself to statements that involve the assumption that other things besides pleasure are desirable, and can be desired. It will be convenient to consider exactly what view it was that Bentham held, in order that the differences that Mill introduced,—the differences involved by his implied belief that other things besides pleasure were desirable—may be brought more clearly into relief.

Bentham held definitely that the only valuable thing in the world was pleasure. Pleasure was therefore the only desirable thing. It was also the only thing actually desired. From this it follows that the mere circumstance of a thing being desired meant that that thing was pleasant, was desirable and was therefore good. Whereas most people would say that there was a distinction between a " desired thing " and a " desirable thing," the distinction being that a desirable thing denotes a thing which ought to be desired in the interests of some standard of morality or some conception of the good, although in point of fact it might not be desired, Bentham held that desired, desirable, and good were interchangeable terms, with identical meanings.

Good therefore has no meaning apart from the amount of pleasure it connotes. Whereas we are familiar with such distinctions as " It is good to go to church, but it is pleasant to stay at home and read novels by the fire," no distinction is involved for Bentham except the distinction between degrees of pleasantness. The one is either more or less pleasant than the other, that is all, and as novels and the fireside are generally regarded as more pleasant than church, it follows not only that we ought to prefer them, for we cannot help preferring the pleasant, but that we inevitably must prefer them and reject church. If in point of fact we do go to church, it proves not that church is regarded as " better," but simply that owing to the curious nature of our desires we happen to find it more pleasant. Two results follow :

1. As we always do what we think will be productive of most pleasure, to say that we ought to do this in preference to that is a meaningless expression ; the word " ought " therefore becomes superfluous. " If the word ought means anything at all it ought to be excluded from the dictionary," was a famous Benthamite motto.

2. As the only criterion of value is pleasantness, it is clear that pleasures cannot differ in quality. They will differ in quantity only. That will be the greater good which is also the more intense pleasure, but we cannot say that one pleasure will be higher than another ; to do so would be to

assume that some other thing besides pleasure, namely height or nobility of pleasure, was valuable. Hence Bentham's famous doctrine, " Quantity of pleasure being equal, push pin is as good as poetry." If our ruler of value is marked out in units of pleasure only, quantity of pleasure is the only thing that we can measure.

Now explicitly this is a position which is adopted by Mill.

As we have seen, he holds that " to think of an object as desirable and to think of it as pleasant are one and the same thing," and " to desire anything, except in proportion as the idea of it is pleasant, is a physical and metaphysical impossibility." We soon, however, find him faltering. He falters in the first place by introducing a distinction of quality in pleasure.

" Of two pleasures . . . if one is, by those who are competently acquainted with both, placed so far above the other that they prefer it, *even though knowing it to be attended with a greater amount of discomfort*, and they would not resign it for any quantity of the other pleasure which their nature is capable of, we are justified in ascribing to the preferred enjoyment a superiority in quality so far outweighing quantity, as to render it in comparison of small account."

Mill goes on to point out that people do as a whole prefer the pleasures attendant upon the exercise of their higher faculties, as compared with a greater quantity of pleasure produced by the indulgence of their lower. A wise man would not consent to be a happy fool ; a person of feeling would not consent to be base, even for a greater share of pleasure, the pleasures namely of the fool and the base. " It is better," says Mill, " to be a human being dissatisfied than a pig satisfied."

This admission is fatal to the position that the only desirable thing is pleasure. If in a whole x, y is the quantity of pleasure, and z the quantity of something other than pleasure, which Mill denotes by the adjective " higher," Mill regards the value of the whole as greater if z is present, than it is if z is absent. But if y, the quantity of pleasure, is the only thing of value, the amount of z present or absent would not affect the value of the whole. It can only affect the whole if z is regarded as possessing value in its own right. If, however, z is regarded as simply pleasure, and not as *higher* pleasure, what is the point of making the distinction in pleasures implied by the word higher? Mill therefore regards certain other things besides pleasure as being desirable, and in so doing gives up the hedonist position in the form in which he professes to hold it, namely that pleasure is the only thing that can be desired.

We come therefore to the second form in which the hedonist position can be asserted, namely that although other things besides pleasure may be desired, pleasure is the only thing that ought to be desired.

We have already seen that in his assertion that people " ought " to desire pleasures of the best or " highest " quality, Mill admitted implicitly that it was possible to desire other things besides sheer pleasure, thus introducing an inconsistency into the pure form of Bentham's doctrine. The inconsistency implicit in his treatment of " quality " of pleasure, is more clearly revealed in Mill's view of the individual's relation to his fellows.

The names of Bentham and Mill are bound up with the famous phrase, " the greatest happiness of the greatest number." The phrase was used as a criterion whereby to assess the rightness or wrongness of actions. An action was right, if it alone of all the other actions possible to the agent at any given moment, tended to produce the most happiness for the most people, and as it was a man's " duty " to do what was right, his duty was always to promote the greatest happiness of the greatest number. But the basis of this so-called " duty " was different for Bentham and for Mill.

Bentham, as we have seen, believed that a human being was so constituted that he could only desire his own greatest possible pleasure or happiness. It follows therefore that it is psychologically impossible for him to desire the greatest happiness of the greatest number, except in so far as the greatest happiness of the greatest number tends to promote his own happiness. Now Bentham believed as a philanthropist that the promotion of the happiness of others was one of the chief sources of personal happiness. He also believed, as a matter of social philosophy, that the net result of the struggle by each individual to attain his own personal pleasure was the imposition by the majority upon the individual of the rule that " every one should count as one and nobody as more than one." The majority impose this rule upon the individual by all the methods of which it has control, by the laws, by the current morality of the time, the press, the pulpit, and the various other organs which go to create that public opinion by which in turn the mind of the individual is moulded. All these organs are directed to impressing upon him the maxim that what produces the general happiness does in the long run produce the greatest happiness for himself.

And as the law stands this maxim is on the whole undeniably true. Abstention from murder and burglary on the part of the individual, produces more happiness for the public than the habitual practice of these pursuits. The community therefore evolves laws and penalties the object of which is to guarantee that such abstention will also conduce to the greater happiness of the individual who abstains.

Hence in saying that right conduct is that which promotes the greatest happiness of the greatest number, Bentham means that such conduct also tends in general to promote our own greatest happiness, and he is therefore perfectly logical on his own premises in calling it right.

If, however, on any particular occasion a certain action which did not promote the general happiness, happened to conduce to the greater happiness of the individual, the individual would on the premises of the hedonistic philosophy be right to perform that action.

Now while Bentham regarded the greatest happiness of the greatest number only as a means to the happiness of the individual, Mill with less logic regarded it as an end in itself.

The principle of utility which he maintains we " ought " to follow, is a principle which does not aim at producing the greatest happiness of the individual, but the greatest happiness of the greatest number. If the happiness of the individual conflicts with this, the individual must go to the wall. " In the golden rule of Jesus of Nazareth we read the complete spirit of the ethics of utility. To do as one would be done by, and to love one's neighbour as oneself, constitute the ideal perfection of utilitarian morality." It is both moral and right therefore to promote the happiness of others. But how can this be if one is so constituted that one can only desire the happiness of oneself ?

Let us suppose that A can, by doing an action P, produce

an amount of happiness X for himself, and an amount of happiness Y for three other people. Let us suppose that by doing another action Q he can produce an amount of happiness C for himself, and an amount of happiness D for three other people. Let us further assume that X is greater than C, and Y is less than D, but that the whole X plus Y is less than the whole C plus D. Then ought A to choose the action P or the action Q ?

According to Mill's first premiss, namely that a man *can* only desire his own greatest happiness, the choice does not arise because A can only choose P, for X is greater than C.

According to his second premiss that a man *ought* always to pursue his own greatest happiness, A ought to choose P on the same ground.

But according to his third premiss that a man ought to promote the greatest happiness of the greatest number, he ought to choose the action Q, on the ground that the total of happiness C plus D is greater than the total X plus Y.

We therefore arrive at the conclusion that Mill does believe that a man ought to pursue something other than his own pleasure, namely the greatest happiness of the greatest number, and furthermore that he ought to pursue it even if it conflicts with his own pleasure.

Now it may be argued that though this is giving up one form of the hedonist position, the form namely which asserts that a man can only desire his own pleasure, it is not giving up the other form of that position, namely that although a man can desire other things besides pleasure, he ought to desire pleasure only ; for by insisting that he ought to desire the greatest happiness of the greatest number, the theory still maintains that pleasure is the only thing that ought to be desired, although it is now somebody else's pleasure.

But in maintaining that the individual ought not to pursue his own pleasure always, but other people's pleasure to the detriment of his own sometimes, we are admitting that something can be and ought to be pursued besides pleasure, namely what is called social good.

We are admitting in fact that the individual can and ought to desire something which may have no relation to his own pleasure, namely the good of the community ; and the mere circumstance that we are for the present identifying that good with pleasure, does not necessarily mean that it is pleasure for the individual. In saying therefore that the individual ought to promote social good or utility, we are in effect saying that it is on occasion his duty to do what may produce pain for himself. The martyr is clearly actuated by such feelings of duty.

We arrive therefore at the conclusion which Mill explicitly denies but implicitly admits, that the individual ought to desire at least one other thing besides his own pleasure, namely social good.

What other things ought to be desired besides pleasure will be considered in the next chapter.

These inconsistencies in Mill are important, and I have dwelt on them at some length because they demonstrate the impracticability of maintaining, even with the best will in the world, that pleasure is the only thing of value. They are liable to occur in any theory which asserts the exclusive value of pleasure, and which attempts to square itself with the facts of human desire. They reveal themselves most completely in Mill's work, but they are implied in any form of Utilitarian hedonism.

It remains to point out two further instances of the departure which Mill makes from the premises of strict hedonism when he attempts to work out his theory, attempts which tend further to emphasize the difficulty of maintaining in detail that happiness is the only thing of value, the only thing which all our actions are intended to promote. A consideration of these departures will therefore pave the way to the conclusions which I shall endeavour to establish in the next chapter, namely that other things besides happiness are valuable.

The first of these instances is afforded by Mill's treatment of virtue. The Utilitarian theory according to Mill does not deny that virtue can be desired. "It maintains not only that virtue is to be desired, but that it is to be desired disinterestedly, for itself." Utilitarians, says Mill, "recognize as a psychological fact the possibility of virtue being, to the individual, a good in itself, without looking to any end beyond it."

This admission seems at first sight to give up the principle that only happiness can be desired altogether. Mill, however, endeavours to reconcile it with his main doctrine, by asserting that though virtue may be desired as an end now, it has only attained this position because it was originally desired as a means, a means, that is, to happiness. People apparently found out that the practice of virtue generally produced happiness, desired virtue for this reason as a means to happiness, and after a time by force of the habit of desiring virtue, forgot the reason for which they originally desired it, and desired it as an end in itself.

But the fact that virtue may once have been desired as a means to an end, does not in the least mean that it is not desired as an end now. The origin of a thing is no invalidation of its present state. To take an instance given by Canon Rashdall: the fact that a savage can only count on the fingers of his two hands, does not invalidate the truth of the multiplication table; and the fact that religion began in devil worship, Totemism, and exogamy, does not mean that it is not religion now.

Similarly the fact that virtue began by being desired for something else, if it is a fact, does not alter the fact that it is desired for itself now; and, if it is so desired, it invalidates the principle that happiness is the only possible object of human desire.

Nor is it an answer to this argument to say as Mill does, that in being desired as an end in itself, virtue is desired " as part of happiness." It is a matter of common observation that so far from always promoting happiness, the practice of virtue very frequently promotes the reverse, and it is not therefore by any means always true that virtue is desired as a part of happiness.

Without attempting accurately to define virtue at this stage, we may note that it can often be identified with the observance of the current code of morality. Novelists and dramatists have made us familiar with the antithesis between virtue in this sense and happiness, and one of the stock conflicts of tragedy, especially in the case of women, is the conflict between the desire to act virtuously, or to preserve one's honour as it is sometimes called on the one hand, and the desire to obtain happiness by following one's affections on the other.

The fact that on the stage the virtuous course usually brings ultimate happiness, is the outcome of the general desire for a " happy ending " which animates those who go to the theatre to be " taken out of themselves "; it is notorious that in its predilection for happy endings melodrama is hopelessly at variance with the facts of life.

It is not therefore by any means always true that virtue is desired as a means to a part of happiness. It is often desired in spite of its demonstrable failure to promote the happiness of any one.

Mill's treatment of justice affords another instance of his failure to subordinate the manifestations of the salient moral faculties to his principle of utility.

The sentiment of justice, according to Mill, has two ingredients: the desire to punish a person who has done harm, and the knowledge or belief that there is some definite individual to whom harm has been done. Of these, the first ingredient arises from two natural sentiments,—the impulse of self-defence, and the feeling of sympathy.

The impulse of self-defence makes us resent wrongs done to ourselves; but this purely egoistic feeling is not yet the principle of justice. It is through the additional feeling of sympathy that man, as distinct from the animals who have the impulse of self-defence only, " is capable of forming a community of interest between himself and the human society of which he forms part." This leads him to resent a harm done to others belonging to his society, just as he resents a harm done to himself. The animal impulse of self-defence is in fact sublimated into a feeling for the good of the society of which the individual forms a part.

This sentiment of resentment at a wrong done to others is in Mill's view at the root of the principle of justice. In asserting this principle the individual is asserting, for the benefit of others, the principle which he would wish to apply to himself. Hence he is asserting the principle of utility in another form, the principle namely, that actions are moral in so far as they promote the greatest happiness of the greatest number.

But if people are able to desire justice, as defined by Mill, it is clear that they are able to desire something which is not only other than their own happiness, but which frequently conflicts with their own happiness.

A man may possess a belonging of his neighbour's. The possession of this belonging may confer upon him very great happiness. The circumstances may be such that it is totally impossible for his neighbour to know that he possesses it : it may also be totally impossible for the present holder to be disturbed in his possession of it : it may also be true that though the rightful owner may get some pleasure from the enjoyment of the belonging, he will not get so much pleasure from it as the man who wrongfully possesses it at the moment. It is clear that in such circumstances the present owner will not, by restoring the belonging, increase the total amount of happiness in the world. His own happiness will be diminished by the loss of the belonging, and this happiness which he loses will not be counter-balanced by the gain in happiness to his neighbour. Nevertheless it would be an act of justice to restore such a belonging, and it is an act which might quite conceivably be performed.

In acting justly therefore men are not always animated by a desire to promote the greatest happiness of the greatest number. Whatever they may desire when acting justly, they do not always desire what Mill's principle of utility says they ought to desire.

Mill's treatment of justice therefore affords another example of the difficulty of maintaining that people do in fact desire or ought in morals to desire pleasure and pleasure only.

§ 4. Summary

It will be convenient to sum up the results to which an examination of the Utilitarian theory has led us.

The Utilitarian theory of Ethics establishes a criterion of right and wrong and makes a judgment of value. The criterion which it asserts is that the rightness and wrongness of actions depend entirely upon the consequences of those actions. They do not depend upon any feeling or set of feelings which any person or body of persons may entertain with regard to them. The validity of this criterion will be discussed in the next chapter. The judgment of value which the Utilitarian theory makes, is that in assessing the consequences by which the rightness or wrongness of actions are to be established, only pleasure or happiness is of value. In so far as this judgment of value is asserted in the form that human beings are so constituted that they can desire nothing but pleasure, we have seen that there are good grounds for believing it to be untrue. In so far as it asserts that people can desire other things besides pleasure, but ought to desire pleasure, we have seen that as treated by its leading exponent, John Stuart Mill, the theory is not held consistently.

In his distinction between the quality of pleasures he implies that other things besides pleasure can and ought to be desired. In his assertion that we ought to promote other people's pleasure even at the expense of our own, he is asserting that we ought to desire the good of society, or in other words that we ought to be altruistic.

In his treatment of virtue and justice his attempts to prove that they are only desired as a means to pleasure, involve a misrepresentation of the ordinary phenomena of moral consciousness, in the course of which he implicitly admits that virtue is desired for its own sake, and justice for the sake of something other than personal pleasure.

In the next chapter it is proposed to discuss the validity of the Utilitarian criterion of right and wrong, and to endeavour to outline a scale of values in contradistinction to the one happiness value. These questions will arise out of a consideration of the Intuitionist theories which in philosophical Ethics are the leading alternative to Utilitarianism.

CHAPTER II

INTUITIONISM AND THE MORAL SENSE

§ 1. The Belief in the Moral Sense

THE criterion laid down by the Utilitarian theory was an objective criterion. It was to the effect that the rightness or wrongness of actions depended on their consequences, that is upon something in the outside world. Many, if not the majority, of philosophers have, however, held that the criterion of rightness and wrongness is subjective. By this is meant that the rightness or wrongness of an action is dependent upon the existence of some sentiment or feeling in some person or body of persons towards that action. Certain actions possess a quality which excites a feeling of approval on the part of what is called the moral sense. This feeling of approval by the moral sense, which is sometimes called an intuition, and is sometimes identified with what is called conscience, is the criterion of rightness and wrongness by which the ethical value of actions is to be measured.

In order to distinguish the Utilitarian from the Intuitionist criterion I propose to call actions judged by the Utilitarian standard right or wrong actions, and actions judged by the Intuitionist standard moral or immoral actions.

A right action then is an action which has the best consequences. A moral action is that which secures the approval of the moral sense.

In saying that an action is moral, we shall mean therefore, among other things, that the approval of the moral sense is in itself alone sufficient to establish its morality, for the moral sense judges actions in themselves, independently of any other consideration such as the consequences they may produce.

The judgments of the moral sense are further ultimate and unanalyzable. The criterion of approval by the moral sense cannot be resolved into anything else. No " why's " can be asked about its judgments, and, according to extreme forms of these theories, no reason need or indeed can be given for its deliverances. Just as our sense of smell is sole and ultimate arbiter in deciding what things smell good and what things smell bad, so our moral sense is ultimate in deciding what actions are moral and what actions are immoral.

In saying that when I affirm an action to be moral, all I mean is that I know it to be moral, or feel it to be moral, or have an intuition to the effect that it is moral, what I am asserting according to these theories is, that no reasons can be asked or given for my feeling or my intuition. This faculty of the moral sense is in fact given to me expressly in order that I may judge actions to be moral or immoral by its means, and it is itself the umpire of its own decisions. There is in short no other faculty by whose means I can judge its deliverances: therefore its deliverances are ultimate.

Before proceeding to consider the nature of the moral sense and the validity of its claim to be the criterion of goodness and badness in matters of conduct, I propose to give a brief outline of the main ethical theories which adopt the moral sense criterion, and to enumerate the different classes of actions of which the ethical value is, according to some one or other of these theories, established by the moral sense.

§ 2. Forms of the Moral Sense Theories

The statement that the moral sense judges actions in themselves independently of other considerations, is not strictly accurate without qualification. In most forms of the theory the moral sense judges those actions to be moral which are done from good motives, or in other words motives of which the moral sense approves.

While the Utilitarians look to the consequences of an action for their judgment upon it, the Intuitionists look to the motive from which it is done.

A moral action is frequently defined therefore as an

action which is done from a moral motive, which is further defined as a motive of which the moral sense approves.

The moral sense theory has been held in a number of different forms, the difference between the forms of the theory consisting mainly in the different types of actions of which the moral sense has been regarded as approving. The variations can, however, be conveniently embraced under three main forms of the theory, the first two of which lay particular emphasis upon motive as being the subject of judgments by the moral sense, the third form being that which regards the moral sense as judging of actions in themselves independently of either motive or consequences.

Kant's Theory of the Free Will

1. The extreme form of that branch of the moral sense theory which holds that the morality of actions depends upon the motive from which they are done was enunciated by the German philosopher, Kant. For Kant, a moral action was that which was done from a sense of duty as opposed to desire.

In considering this view it will be necessary to say a few words about the relation between reason and desire.

Most philosophers have held that the mainspring of all action was desire. In Aristotle's view, desire sets the end as a whole: it also formulates all the petty individual ends, the achievement of which is but a step on the road to the achievement of the end as a whole. The individual's desires are, however, apt to be a chaotic, unruly band each of which clamours for satisfaction for itself at the expense of the others. If, for instance, I desire at the same time to go to bed, and to sit up and read Meredith, it is clear that the one desire can only be satisfied at the expense of the other. But the satisfaction of one of these two desires will also be more conducive to the realization of the end as a whole than the satisfaction of the other.

We have, therefore, according to Aristotle, over and above the competitive desires which are self-regarding and neglectful of the good of the whole, a desire for the end as a whole whose business it is to discipline the individual desires, to dovetail each into its special place in the whole structure, and to permit it only that amount of satisfaction which is compatible with the good of the whole.

This desire for the good of the whole Aristotle called the Will. The function of reason is to ascertain the various steps by which the achievement of the end of each desire and of the whole can be realized, and to devise how those steps may be taken. Reason is then the servant of desire, and also of the will which desires the good of the whole.

Action which is dictated by will or by the desire for the good of the whole, is, according to Aristotle, moral action.

I have briefly summarized Aristotle's account of moral action, in order that the position taken up by Kant may be more clearly defined by contrast.

According to Kant not only was it possible for an individual to act as the result of the promptings of reason as opposed to desire, but he could only be regarded as acting freely when he acted from reason and not from desire. This view depends upon Kant's peculiar notion of freedom.

Kant conceived of man alone in nature as being free, that is exempt from the laws of cause and effect which prevail throughout nature. "Everything in nature works according to laws. Rational beings alone have the faculty of acting according to the *conception* of laws—that is according to principle, in other words, to have a will."

When acting in accordance with will which is rational, man is acting according to the laws of his own nature : he is therefore acting freely and morally. But man does not consist of reason only. He is a sentient being, sharing the life of sentient creation and as such influenced by the external stimuli which produce pain and pleasure. When man allows these stimuli to dictate his actions, he is acting according to desire. Hence arises a conflict between action according to desire stimulated from outside, and action dictated by reason, which has its seat within, and works through the will. Action of this latter type only is moral and really free. The only things in the world of moral value, said Kant, are a free will and the actions which spring from it. The free will is the result of man's power of self-determination, as opposed to determination from outside, and, according to Kant, extorts unconditional allegiance in the performance of certain actions. Kant's famous phrase,

INTUITIONISM AND THE MORAL SENSE

the " categorical imperative," is used to denote the binding nature of the obligation which the rational will lays upon human beings to act only in accordance with its dictates. In so far as they act in accordance with desire men are acting immorally. The morality of actions depends therefore upon the circumstances which determine the action.

" An action done from a sense of duty derives its moral worth not from the purpose which is to be attained by it, but from the maxim by which it is determined, and therefore does not depend on the realization of the object of the action, but merely upon the principle of volition by which the action has taken place, without regard to any object of desire."

Kant's ethical philosophy therefore makes the goodness or badness of an action depend upon some occurrence in the psychology or mental state of the agent. The action is good or moral if it is the result of the dictates of the rational will, immoral if it is the result of desire occasioned by external stimuli.

Bringing this statement under the formula of motive which we began by using, we shall say that the kind of motive upon which the goodness of an action depends, according to Kant, is the motive engendered by the operations of the free will.

The first of the classes of actions therefore of which the moral sense has been historically regarded by philosophers as approving, is the class of actions that spring from that kind of motive known as the free will.

The Morality of Motive

2. There are, however, other actions belonging to that class of actions whose goodness is regarded by philosophers as depending upon their being done from a motive of which the moral sense approves, which do not involve the extreme view of the relation between reason and desire held by Kant as their basis.

The motive criterion as the standard for the measurement of the rightness and wrongness of action is the chief bogey writers like Mill are endeavouring to dispel, in their insistence that the criterion must be found in the consequences of the action. Many writers have insisted that the motive from which the action was done was the main factor in determining its rightness or wrongness. Bishop Butler, for instance, who believed in the unique and unanalyzable character of the moral motive held that " the rightness or wrongness of an act depends very much upon the motive for which it is done." Few of these writers, however, go to the length of Kant in making the morality of action depend entirely upon motive and not at all upon consequences, and an endeavour is made to disarm the Utilitarians and to gain the advantages of their position by asserting that motive and consequences cannot be divorced from one another as two distinct and unrelated things, that they are inalienably connected, and that the moral sense in approving actions done from a moral motive, is also bestowing its approval upon actions which produce good consequences. This is the line which is taken for instance by such writers as Professor Muirhead in his book, " The Elements of Ethics."

How is this intimate connection between motive and consequences made out ?

The word motive is a complex word, involving at least two different elements. One of these is feeling, and this factor of feeling is of great importance. Aristotle's position that feeling is the mainspring of all action has, as a general rule, been accepted by philosophers, and there can be little doubt that on this point Aristotle was right. This element of feeling is usually a form of desire. The pleasure seeker must, in doing an action which he intends to bring him pleasure, experience a desire for the pleasure before he can perform the action. Scientific experimenters are prompted by a feeling of curiosity, or by the desire for the discovery of truth that may result from the experiment. Purely impulsive actions, like the withdrawal of the finger from a poker which proves unexpectedly hot, though not prompted by a desire for any ulterior end to be gained by the action, are nevertheless occasioned by a feeling of pain. If the feeling were not there we should suffer our finger to remain on the poker.

Feeling then is a conditioning factor in all action, the engine which supplies the steam that sets the mechanism of action in motion. But feeling by itself is not the only element in what is called motive. Motive implies as a rule

INTUITIONISM AND THE MORAL SENSE 27

an end or an aim, the picturing or presentation to oneself of the results of the action which it prompts.

For the purposes of this consideration of motive actions may be divided into two classes: those which are purely impulsive, and those in which the agent sets before himself an object or end to be attained as the result of his action.

Actions of the first class are as a rule the automatic results of excitation by external stimuli. The withdrawal of the hand from the red-hot poker, or the shutting of the eye when a fly enters it, are conditioned entirely by something outside the agent. They are not the products of the individual's will, nor are they prompted by any motive in the sense in which we have been using the word. It seems doubtful therefore whether they can be described as voluntary actions, in the sense in which actions which are done for the sake of a definite object are voluntary, and, if this is the case, they cannot be regarded as proper subjects either for the approval or disapproval of the moral sense. They are morally neutral.

Actions of the other class, however, are voluntary, being undertaken for the sake of a definite end or purpose, and the idea of this end cannot, it is argued, be distinguished from the motive which prompts the action. The will or motive to perform an action of this class contains an idea of the consequences expected therefrom, and, inasmuch as it inevitably points forward to those consequences and takes its shape and quality from them, cannot be judged apart from them. When the moral sense approves therefore of actions done from a good motive, it is not making a judgment about motive alone divorced from the consequences of the action, motive so divorced being meaningless, but it includes in its scope the end towards which the motived action is directed, from the nature of which end the motive takes its colour. In saying, in short, that the motive which leads people to torture animals is bad, the moral sense does so mainly if not wholly because the results of the action in question, namely the pain experienced by the animal, are bad, and the motive of an act which is expected to produce pain derives its nature from the consequences it contemplates.

Although, in admitting that the consequences of actions are a factor which the criterion of right and wrong must take into account, this form of the " moral sense " theories is in agreement with the Utilitarians an important distinction between the two views must be noted.

When it holds that a judgment of motives involves a judgment of consequences, the moral sense view means the expected consequences. When the Utilitarian asserts that the rightness or wrongness of actions must be judged by their consequences, he means their actual consequences whether intended or not. This is a real difference. Before pointing out its significance, however, it is necessary to explain a little more fully what is meant by expected consequences.

When it is said that motive takes its colour from the expected consequences of the action it prompts, the ultimate or final consequences of the action are meant. These must be distinguished from the immediate consequences, although these are in an equal degree intended and expected. Thus if a dentist uses a drill to stop a tooth, the immediate expected consequences are painful and unpleasant, although the ultimate expected consequences are beneficial. When the moral sense approves the motive of the dentist's action as taking its colour from the aim the dentist sets before himself, the expected ultimate consequences are the grounds of its approval, not the immediate painful ones. Yet the immediate painful consequences are equally expected and equally intended. In order to maintain this distinction Bentham defines motive as that for the sake of which an action is done; whereas intention includes both that for the sake of which and that in spite of which an action is done. Intention is therefore wider than motive, and of the total sum of the intended or expected consequences only those for the sake of which the action is done form the subject of approval or disapproval by the moral sense.

Returning to the distinction between this form of the moral sense criterion and the Utilitarian criterion, it is obvious that the intended or expected consequences of an action are very different from the actual consequences. Nobody can ever know *all* the actual consequences of an action, and for this reason alone it is impossible to say whether the intended consequences are identical with them.

Frequently, however, it is obvious that they are very different. This difference is especially marked in the case of well-meaning, interfering people who are so anxious to avoid giving pain that they can be relied on in an emergency to make everybody suffer.

Let us suppose that A is an action of which the actual consequences are X and the expected consequences are Y; and let us further suppose that X are bad and Y are good. Then A is an action which is a wrong action by the Utilitarian standard, although it is a moral action by the moral sense standard.

A possible line of reconciliation between the two views will be considered in the fourth chapter: for the present, however, it is sufficient to note that we have now arrived at a second class of actions of which the moral sense has been historically regarded as approving, those namely done from a moral motive, a motive which takes its colour from the expected consequences of the action and cannot be divorced from them.

Conscience as an Unique Faculty

3. It will be remembered that we have defined a moral motive as that of which the moral sense approves. What are the grounds for this approval?

The answer to this question leads us to a consideration of the third class of actions of which the moral sense has been regarded as approving, a class of actions which can only be defined from the circumstance that the moral sense approves of them. If we ask for the grounds of its approval, either of moral motives or of this third class of actions, the answer is that there are none. The dictates of the moral sense are regarded on this view as ultimate and unanalyzable, and it is as unreasonable to ask why the moral sense approves as to ask why we approve of health, or like music, or dislike the smell of castor oil: we just do. What are the reasons for this view?

It is held in the first place that the moral sense is a unique faculty which we possess, whose function it is to pass judgments which are valid in their own right. With regard to the exact composition of this faculty there has been dispute. Some writers, like Bishop Butler and an ethical philosopher named Martineau, have regarded it as a distinct and unique part of our natures, uncompounded of other ingredients, which reigns over the sphere of conduct and morals, just as the sense of taste is the arbiter of flavours, and the sense of hearing the judge of music. In this form it is usually spoken of as conscience.

Other writers regard it as a kind of feeling, others again as a manifestation of reason, most perhaps as a sort of composite fusion of reason and emotion, entitled, in order to save the difficulty of more precise definition, by the question-begging word of "Intuition." The dash of reason in Intuition gives it more authority than a mere feeling: the dash of instinct gives it a mysterious rapidity and directness of operation, so that it comes to be regarded as a short cut to the truth, of unerring aim and rapid flight, a charming alternative to the ponderous perambulations of heavy-footed reason. It is sometimes, though not often, admitted that like other short cuts it may just as likely land its followers in the ditch.

Whatever the nature of this faculty, it is held that it gives immediate assent to certain moral propositions, of the truth of which no guarantee is required, further than the fact of the assent being given. Just as the rational faculty immediately realizes that the proposition $2 + 2 = 4$ is true, so the moral sense instinctively apprehends the truth of propositions such as "It is better to promote happiness than pain." If anybody fails to subscribe to the truth of this proposition he is devoid of the moral sense, and to that extent not wholly a human being.

The deliverances of this sense take the form of immediate judgments that certain actions or classes of actions are right and wrong, irrespective of their consequences. Certain actions win the approval of the moral sense because they are like that and because the moral sense is like that, and that is all there is about it. In the words of Bishop Butler, "There is something as yet darkly known which makes right right and wrong wrong."

The deliverances of the moral sense are clearest and most unanimous in regard to propositions in very general terms, such as, "Kindness is better than unkindness"; "All lying is wrong"; "All stealing is wrong"; "Honesty is better than dishonesty." It is further claimed by some, but with less confidence, that these intuitions or deliverances of the moral sense apply with equal unerringness to particular actions, issuing in judgments such as, "It is wrong to tell this particular lie," "That particular business transaction is shady," these judgments being pronounced without reference to consequences and remaining valid, even if the consequences of disapproved actions unexpectedly prove to be beneficial.

It is argued in support of this view that the belief in morality as a good in itself without reference to any ulterior end is one of the strongest beliefs that we possess. That although the performance of good actions does as a fact usually produce satisfaction, yet virtue is regarded as an end in itself, and is pursued as such independently of its value as a means to pleasure or self-satisfaction. That intuitions of this kind are possessed by children, who, although they have not been instructed in their elders' code of morality, almost invariably know that lying is wrong, and have a sense of guilt when they have told a lie, even when they are not afraid of being found out or of being punished if they are found out.

Psycho-analysts have pointed out that children who suffer from some form of sexual perversion invariably feel a sense of guilt which makes them disguise its manifestations, although from the very oddity and irrelevance of the form of the perversion, it is most unlikely that they have ever been told that it was wrong. To take a common enough instance, a boy finds that it gives him intense pleasure of a sexual character to squeeze his feet into boots that are too small for him. Clearly nobody has ever told him that such a proceeding was wrong; yet cases are historically recorded in which boys so affected have admitted that they knew such actions to be immoral, have performed them furtively, and in doing so have experienced all those feelings of loss of self-respect commonly associated with what in Christian terminology is known as yielding to temptation.

Furthermore these inalienable judgments with regard to the rightness and wrongness of particular actions or classes of actions, are exercised perhaps in the most marked degree by uneducated and illiterate persons, who have neither the wit nor the interest to care about the consequences of the actions they approve or condemn, or about their social effects.

A keen moral sense is often found conjoined with little knowledge of the world, and practically no capacity for accounting for or justifying its dictates; and people who unhesitatingly condemn stealing as immoral, are often completely at a loss to give any reason for their judgment or to explain why a society of burglars is less to be desired than a society of middle-class persons who spend their time in feverishly respecting one another's property, and all being moral together. If therefore the moral sense judgment is not based upon an estimate of the consequences of actions, it must, for lack of anything else to which it may attach itself, be a judgment passed about the actions themselves.

Thus we arrive at a third class of actions which the moral sense has been regarded as approving or disapproving, this class consisting of certain specific actions and types of actions which can be defined neither by motive nor by consequences, nor indeed by any distinguishing mark other than the circumstance of their being those particular actions of which the moral sense approves or disapproves.

All three types of actions, which we have been considering, those done from a Kantian free will, those done from a motive other than a Kantian free will of which the moral sense approves, and certain specific actions approved in themselves by the moral sense, have this in common, that their goodness is regarded as dependent upon the fact of the moral sense passing a judgment of approval upon them. The criterion of their goodness consists therefore not in the nature of their consequences, but in the nature of the feelings entertained towards them by some person or body of persons, the word feeling being used here in a wide and loose sense to describe the functioning of the moral sense.

We have now to see what are the arguments which can be brought against the moral sense theory in any of the three main forms in which we have been considering it, and whether these same arguments should lead us to prefer that alternative theory of the criterion of morality which we considered in the first chapter, that is the Utilitarian criterion which makes the rightness or wrongness of actions depend upon their consequences.

This line of inquiry will also lead us to the question which was left undiscussed in the first chapter, namely whether the Utilitarian theory was right in its assertion that in assessing the consequences of action the only thing that is of ultimate value is happiness.

INTUITIONISM AND THE MORAL SENSE

§ 3. Criticism of the Moral Sense Theories

The objections which may be brought against the Intuitionist or moral sense theories enumerated above are of a serious and, to my mind, of a convincing character.

Some of them were first used by the Utilitarians in the early part of the nineteenth century when the contention between the two schools of thought was keenest. Most of them were enunciated in some form or other by Sidgwick in his famous book "The Method of Ethics."

I do not propose to go in very great detail into these objections, as I hold that in a very real sense, which will be explained later, the points at issue between the Intuitionist and Utilitarian Schools are purely academic, but will summarize as briefly as possible the main arguments upon which the objections are based.

These arguments may be most conveniently summarized under five heads. The first two apply only to the last of the three main forms of the moral sense theory described above, while the last three apply equally to each of the three forms in which that theory has been asserted.

Conflicting Dictates of the Moral Sense

1. In the last form in which we considered the moral sense theory, the moral sense was regarded as supplying us with immediate judgments of approval or disapproval, sometimes called intuitions, with regard to classes of actions or particular actions.

In so far as the existence of these intuitions with regard to particular actions is asserted, the proposition may with reason be flatly denied.

Although there may be a kind of vague consensus of opinion among most people in most periods of the world's history with regard to certain classes of actions, as for instance a fairly general disapproval of lying, there is almost invariably the greatest possible disagreement between people's intuitions about particular actions.

The conflict between the opinions of two apparently morally-minded people as to the right course of action under a particular set of circumstances is one of the stock subjects of tragedy and drama, and need not be enlarged upon.

Only it should be noted that as a moral action is, upon this theory, one with regard to which a feeling of approval is entertained by the moral sense, it is impossible to regard both the disputants whose moral senses disagree as equally right. To do so would involve the assumption that the same action is both moral and immoral at the same time, make rightness and wrongness a question of taste, like the sweetness of meringues, and so destroy that foundation of objectivity for moral judgments upon which this school so confidently bases the validity of its intuitions. Not only do people have different intuitions with regard to the morality of the same action, but the moral sense most noticeably fails to deliver itself of any judgment at all when clamorously required to do so. The path of duty is often as hard to find as it is to follow. Hamlet is not so much a man torn by conflicting duties, as one who turns an anxious ear to the voice of a conscience, which persistently fails to respond even by the vaguest hint of the course which ought to be pursued.

The judgments of the moral sense are thus neither unanimous nor unfailing. Intuitions, if they are to be valid and not the mere deliverances of irresponsible instinct, should be both. Not even with regard to classes of actions does the moral sense deliver itself in unmistakable terms. Spartan children were taught to steal; chastity was unknown among the Turks, truth among the Cretans: yet it is surely in the case of general maxims with regard to property and sex that the voice of the moral sense should be unfaltering and its manifestations constant.

Most significant of all is the fact that where people do differ with regard to the morality of particular actions, or nations with regard to the morality of particular codes of conventional conduct, it is always by an appeal to *the consequences* of the action or class of actions that one side invokes superiority for its own particular judgment as opposed to that of its neighbours.

Actions Divorced from Consequences

2. In assuming that actions divested of their consequences form the subject of judgments by the moral sense, this form of the moral sense theory errs in supposing they can be so divested.

INTUITIONISM AND THE MORAL SENSE

What would be wrong with stealing if it did not lead to want, insecurity, remorse and unhappiness? Divested of these consequences it would cease to be stealing.

"What would be the sense," says Canon Rashdall, "of asking whether drunkenness would still be wrong if it did not make a man thick in his speech, unsteady in his gait, erratic in his conduct, incoherent in his thoughts, and so on?"

Actions stripped of their consequences are meaningless. They have no more ethical significance than the workings of an automaton: in fact they cannot be so stripped.

Unfortunate Consequences of Moral Actions

3. Once the factor of consequences is taken into account, it must be noted that actions which are shown to be moral, on either of the three forms of the moral sense theory frequently have the *worst* possible consequences.

In using the phrase "worst consequences" at this stage of our inquiry I am not endeavouring to beg one of the main questions which I have set out to discuss, the question namely of what is the meaning of the word bad as applied to consequences. It will be remembered that, according to the theory considered in the first chapter, the badness of the consequences resulting from an action renders the action which produces those consequences a wrong action; but it was left an open question at the end of the chapter whether "worst" consequences meant solely those which consisted of the maximum amount of unhappiness possible, or whether there were other things besides happiness which possessed elements of intrinsic value, and which must be taken into account in estimating the goodness or badness of consequences. For the present it will be sufficient to point out that happiness has been regarded practically universally as a good or desirable thing, even if it is not the only good, and that we saw reason in the first chapter to doubt whether any whole could be regarded as valuable unless it contained at least some happiness.

Whatever else the phrase "worst consequences" may mean therefore, it is clear that it will mean among other things, consequences which involve a minimum quantity of happiness and which also involve a considerable amount of unhappiness or pain.

Yet many actions which are done from a moral motive, or from a free will in Kant's sense of the phrase, or which are regarded as moral in themselves, do frequently have consequences of this character.

In certain Greek city States the exposure of unwanted infants was regarded as a highly moral and patriotic duty. Whatever amount of social good such a measure may have involved, or however commendable it may have been on Nietzschean principles, it is clear that it did not conduce to the happiness either of the mothers or of the infants.

Similarly the burning of witches in the Middle Ages was regarded as a highly moral and even religious act: it was also defended on moral grounds by writers who make no pretensions either to religious enthusiasm or to religious prejudice. Yet the consequences clearly involved unhappiness for the witches, and although it may be argued that they involved an even greater amount of happiness for the onlookers who had the satisfaction of beholding the discomfiture of those whom they feared or disliked, and of debauching that morbid lust for horrors which makes most of us revel in books of tortures and in Madame Tussaud's, it is equally clear that it is not on this ground that they were defended.

All wars declared by States, nations or tribes have been undertaken from professedly moral motives and defended on professedly moral grounds: it is even possible that in some cases they *have* been undertaken from moral motives and defended on moral grounds. Their consequences have, however, been uniformly bad in the sense provisionally defined above.

Now it is clear that the fact that actions of this class do have bad consequences does not disprove the fact that the moral sense of many people passes a judgment of approval upon them. It does, however, afford a very strong presumption for doubting the theory which holds that the passing of the judgment of approval by the moral sense is in itself a sufficient criterion of the morality of actions, that the moral sense is, in fact, infallible.

In the case of actions of the kind described above, the moral sense of many people passes an equally clear judgment of disapproval upon the consequences of the actions which in themselves have gained the approval of the moral sense of many.

Now the fact of one judgment being passed about the consequences of an action while a contrary judgment is passed upon the action itself, taken in conjunction with the difficulty attending any attempt to divorce an action from its consequences, means in effect that the same actions are at once the object of judgments of approval and of disapproval by the moral sense.

In any event we arrive at the conclusion that the mere passing of a judgment by the moral sense upon either an action or its consequences is not in itself sufficient to establish the rightness or wrongness of the action.

This objection applies both to actions whose intended consequences are good,—and whose motive therefore wins the approval of the moral sense,—but whose actual consequences are bad, and to those actions which are judged good in themselves by direct intuitions.

The Relation of the Moral Sense to Society

4. Not only does the moral sense of different people pass contradictory judgments upon the same action at the same time, but the moral sense of the same communities at different times, instead of being a fixed, definite and infallible thing, as supporters of the theory would have us believe, is constantly changing, while the moral sense of different communities at the same period is frequently contradictory. The Greek historian Herodotus makes a sage remark to the effect that while fires burn upwards in all parts of the world, people's notions of right and wrong are everywhere different, whence the stability of natural and the mutability of moral phenomena are inferred.

Canon Rashdall estimates that "There is hardly a vice or a crime (according to our own moral standard) which has not at some time or other, in some circumstances, been looked upon as a moral or religious duty."

Instances have been given above of the approval bestowed by the moral sense upon actions which, having regard to their consequences, can only be described as outrageous.

It has also bestowed approval upon actions which may be fairly termed ridiculous. Our Victorian ancestors insisted on swathing the legs of their grand pianos on the ground that being legs they were necessarily indecent. The monks on Mount Athos carried the early Christian prejudice against the female sex to such lengths that they devoted much time and labour to devising a method for producing eggs without keeping hens. It may fairly be argued then that the deliverances of the moral sense are frequently too misleading, contradictory and even trivial in their nature to form a reliable criterion of right or wrong. As they are constantly changing, they involve the assumption that the same action which is right in one age is wrong in another; as they are constantly contradictory, they involve the assumption that the same action is both right and wrong at the same time.

But the moral sense view is not so readily to be disposed of as these arguments might at first suggest. In the first place attempts are made to show that the deliverances of the moral sense are not as irresponsible as they appear, by pointing to the fact that they are usually directed to the maintenance of order and the preservation of the social structure of the time. In the second place it is also urged that a definite trend of progress can be observed in the changes of the standard set by the moral sense, and that the moral judgments of succeeding races which have played a prominent part in history show a continuous advance.

The first of these contentions is in the main a true one and raises an important point. Dealing with the problem presented by the relativity of moral judgments, Professor Muirhead points out that morality does not consist in obedience to a fixed code of rules. The rules change, and they are different for different individuals. They change because different societies are differently constituted. They are different for different individuals, because individuals have different stations in society. The individual is a social unit: he cannot be considered as an isolated entity. Morality consists in relations with one's fellows, and the individual has a definite rôle to play and status to maintain in society. As a social being therefore his duty is relative to his station and circumstances.

Now states and societies evolve: therefore morality which contains a " quality of social tissue " must evolve with them. It varies with reference to the needs of society, and the morality of any society, finding concrete expression in the laws, prescribes as moral whatever contributes to the maintenance of that society, and allocates to the individual his proper place within it. The judgments of the moral sense are therefore relative to the needs of society: that does not mean, however, that they are not binding. "It is because," says Professor Muirhead, "morality is always and in all places relative to circumstances, that it is binding at any time and in any place."

But this position is open to an objection which is mentioned in passing by Professor Muirhead himself, but of which he does not appear to recognize the full force.

Supposing for a moment we assume that the standard of morality *is* relative to the needs and nature of society, and that changes in the deliverances of the moral sense are occasioned, and rightly occasioned by changes in the social forms under which the individual lives and by which his moral standards are moulded.

We have indeed gained this much, that we have shown that the variations in the moral standard are not purely irresponsible, but exhibit a common quality or principle of unity in that they are related to and conditioned by changes in society. We are further enabled to define morality as that kind of conduct which at any given moment supports and maintains the particular social form to which society has evolved.

But what are we to say of the evolution of society? It it purposive and designed? Does it exhibit progress? Can we say of every particular stage of society that it ought to be maintained, because it is more advanced than the last? Can we in fact discover in the history of the human race a standard of progressive good, by reference to which we can at last claim an absolute validity for our moral standard, on the ground that it is concerned to support and maintain the progressively evolving stages of the human race?

This question, which brings us to the second point which can be made in defence of the validity of moral judgments, is an important one. If changes in society are arbitrary and irresponsible, then the code of morality which supports them is equally irresponsible. If evolution does not involve an ethical advance, then the deliverances of the moral sense which approve of the stage of evolution which has at any moment been reached, are themselves devoid of that ultimate validity which a discernible relation to human good can alone bestow. Morality becomes, in Professor Muirhead's words, "nothing but that kind of conduct which supports one or other of the accidental changes in the phantasmagoria of social forms."

By recognizing in short that the moral sense is relative, we have transferred the whole burden of making good a claim to absolute validity from the moral sense to the social structure to which it is relative. If a standard of progress can be observed in the evolution of society, then a similar standard can immediately be established for the moral sense which registers each stage in the advance with the mark of its approval. If, however, no such progress can be discerned the moral sense will gain neither in significance nor in validity from the fact that it automatically confers approval upon acts tending to maintain existing social forms, and will become merely an instrument for bolstering up the State because it exists, blindly lending its support to the bad as well as to the good.

The question of whether the structure of the universe exhibits design and purpose, and whether the changes of society can be regarded as the expression of this purpose, brings us to the threshold of metaphysics which it is at all times difficult to exclude from ethical discussion. Some of the questions which are involved will be treated more fully in the last chapter, but at this stage it will be sufficient to advance certain considerations which tend to throw doubt upon this attempt to legitimize the promptings of the moral sense by relating them to the alleged progressive evolution of society, without for the present taking up any definite attitude with regard to the vexed question of purpose and design in the Universe.

The Moral Sense as the Pillar of the State

(i) In the first place it is necessary to point out that the function of the moral sense in acting as a sort of pillar of society is not in itself sufficient to invest it with validity. Many societies are definitely bad societies according to any reasonable criterion of political valuation that one may

INTUITIONISM AND THE MORAL SENSE

choose to invoke, and the moral sense that counsels obedience to their laws is infected with the evil of what it upholds. In particular it should be noticed that it is a characteristic of the moral sense to approve of conduct which is legitimized by the laws, and to disapprove of whatever is inimical to that order in the State which it is one of the functions of law to maintain.

Yet the State which is responsible for the maintenance of law and order may be a repressive and coercive force, and the attempt to subvert instead of to uphold the institutions under which we live may therefore be a desirable expression of the desire for liberty. When the State is tyrannical, the moral sense should act as an incentive to revolt, instead of being a sort of adjunct to the State police force. Yet the theory which attempts to define the moral sense as the upholder of society would allot to it the performance of the latter function only, and would regard the former with the horror and distaste which people who profit by the *status quo* usually feel for efforts on the part of those they oppress to subvert the State.

It is significant that most Socialist political theory regards almost every form of society which has hitherto existed as a device for oppressing the mass of the people, and enabling the privileged few to maintain themselves on the fruits of the labour of others. Karl Marx, for instance, regarded the State as an organization of the exploiting class, for maintaining the conditions of exploitation that suit it, and held that the moral sense of the proletariat was deliberately moulded and perverted by the capitalists into an acceptance of those regulations and institutions which secure to the latter the surplus value of the labour of the former. Those who adopt this view must necessarily regard the moral sense not as a force of progress, but as one of the most powerful instruments of oppression. The exploitation of the religious sense by those who inculcate the practice of the Christian virtues of humility and contentment because their observance by the poor makes for undisturbed possession by the rich, may be cited as a parallel.

It is not necessary for us to subscribe in all cases to these extreme views as to the nature of the State, the utility of Christianity to the rich, and its consequent popularization among the poor, to recognize clearly that the value of any existing form of social organization is not sufficiently established to enable us to claim validity for the deliverances of the moral sense, solely in virtue of the rôle it plays in maintaining and supporting existing forms of social structure.[1]

The assumption of progress in the successive forms of human evolution is therefore essential to the legitimizing of the moral sense as a criterion of right and wrong.

We must be in a position to show that each stage of evolution constitutes a definite advance upon its predecessor, that man is not only later than, but higher than the amœba, and that in the history of specifically human organizations the various forms which society has assumed succeed one another not only in time, but also in advancement.

The Dogma of Progress in Morals and Society

(ii) Can this assumption be made? Most writers on Ethics are of opinion that it can, and this opinion lies at the basis of their confidence in the moral sense.

Professor Muirhead, whose views on this point may be regarded as fairly typical, cites from Herbert Spencer the formula for progress in evolution: "Evolution is a process whereby an indefinite, incoherent homogeneity is transformed into a definite, coherent heterogeneity."

Thus the jelly-fish is, with minor qualifications, structureless and homogeneous: man is a vertebrate of a highly complicated character, his bones being clearly of a different substance from his brains, and his alleged soul. Similarly in primitive societies all men lead the same kind of life, and the social structure is simple: in so-called civilized societies one man lives in a mine, and another inhabits a mansion, while society is cut across by an infinitely diverse stratification composed of divisions mainly of wealth, partly of blood, and to a smaller extent of intelligence.

That the process by which the structureless jelly-fish evolves into the highly complex and differentiated human being is a form of progress is taken so much for granted that it is not generally thought necessary to adduce any evidence in support of this belief.

[1] I shall return to the question of the relation between the moral sense and any existing form of Government in Chapter VI.

With regard to the evolution of society there is indeed ample evidence for the gradually increasing complexity both of form and function. Comte traces the development from what he calls the Fetichist period when the elements of family life and primitive ideas of property were the main characteristics of society; though what he calls the Polytheistic period of the Greek city States, which show a higher degree of complexity of laws and institutions, to the Roman world in which law becomes at once more detailed and embracing, and the divisions into classes more numerous.

This increase of heterogeneity is, according to this view, accompanied by a moral advance. The Roman world established for the first time a widespread reign of law and security. With the feudal era and the spread of Christianity, slaves are emancipated and become serfs, who in their turn become the free labourers of the industrial era. The slavery of the wage system, whereby a man has no choice but to sell his labour to the owners of the instruments of production, in order that he may live, being a slavery not of law but only of fact, apparently escapes notice.

With this advance in diversity of social structure comes an increasing diversity and elaboration of the moral code. The traditional moral customs of the barbarians and early Greeks become the highly elaborate and rational morality of the Greek philosophers. The general principles laid down in the Ten Commandments become particularized into the Book of the Covenant. The somewhat primitive and vindictive morality which animates the heroes of the Old Testament is refined into the highly spiritualized moral code of the Sermon on the Mount.

It would be superfluous to increase the instances. The process by which society becomes more complex and moral codes more elaborate is sufficiently obvious. Nor are the two developments disconnected. If, as has been argued, what gets itself called moral, is the sort of conduct which maintains existing institutions, it is clear that the moral sense will have more scope for its deliverances as the number of institutions increase in quantity; if the social organism is differentiated into an ever increasing diversity of forms and classes; it is clear that the number of moral codes, each appropriate to a particular class and relative to its position and status in the whole organism, will grow in proportion. The progress of growing heterogeneity is admitted. The question is, can it justly be termed progress ?

Anything like an adequate consideration of this question would involve a more extensive trespassing on the preserves of metaphysics than has been undertaken up to the present, or than it would be desirable to undertake at this stage.

Some of the questions which it involves are : is there a discernible purpose in the Universe ; is that purpose making for good ; is it embodied and expressed in human institutions ?

Even if we admit that the growing heterogeneity observable, as evolution proceeds, both in the structure of the human form and of social institutions, is accompanied by an enrichment and enlargement of the moral standard, and that the growing complexity both in human institutions and in the moral sense which supports them can be called progress, there still remains the question of whether the process is subject to natural laws, so that each stage of it is mechanically determined from without, or whether it can be regarded as the continuous striving of a self-conscious intelligence to express itself in the system of social relations and institutions which we call human society.

Is the process we have described, even if it be termed progress, inevitably conditioned by mechanical laws, like the apple which falls from the tree, or is it an expression of the fundamental nature of human consciousness, a product of human will, which is itself an expression of the divine nature that made the world ?

It is intended to give some consideration to these questions in the last chapter of this book. For the present it will be sufficient to point out that until they have received some sort of answer, the affirmation of the principle of progress in human society and in the moral standard which registers each alleged advance in the social structure with its approval, is not in itself sufficient to endow the deliverances of the moral sense with that validity which is required if they are to form an adequate criterion of right and wrong. If in short the progress is mechanically conditioned by the operation of natural laws, so is the moral sense which keeps time with it, and the principle of morality will not be an expression of human or divine consciousness, but merely a natural development determined by outside circumstances, like the shedding of our tails, or the atrophying of our appendices, similar in kind to and possessing no more authority than any other instinct. With this proviso we can proceed to consider how far the existence of progress both in man and in the societies he has formed can be substantiated.

Without going at length into this intricate question, I wish to point out three considerations which seem to me to rob the principle of progress of much of the certainty which is claimed for it.

Change and Progress not Identical

(ii) (a) Let us assume that the continuous evolutionary development which biologists record from the amoeba to the human being is an established fact. When the researches of Darwin and his followers showed that human life, instead of being unique in the catalogue of natural phenomena, a fresh creation, as it were, endowed with a nature which in virtue of its rational and perhaps also of its spiritual characteristics removed it by an impassible gulf from the lower animals, had been gradually evolved as the result of a continuous process involving intermediate beings who could not with certainty be classed as members either of the animal or the human species, the blow delivered to human conceit was at first staggering. And later biologists, though differing with regard to the manner of evolution, tending to regard it as a process of discontinuous jumps rather than a gradual modification of existing species, have not thrown doubt on the central fact that human nature has been evolved.

Human nature, however, quickly found its way to reassert its self-respect by investing the process of evolution with ethical considerations. The process which transformed the amoeba into the ape and the ape into the human being quickly came to be regarded not only as a process but as a progress. But in making the assertion that change in structure and development in time, involved change in value and development in morals, thinkers have gone entirely beyond the evidence.

" A process which led from the amoeba to man," says Mr. Bertrand Russell, " appeared to the philosophers to be obviously a progress, though whether the amœba would agree with this opinion is not known." Until we can obtain the views of the amœba, until further we can arrive at some agreement as to the goal to be attained, and the standard of value by which we are to measure, it is not possible either to affirm progress or to deny it.

I do not mean that the change has not involved progress: I am only asserting that on our present evidence we are not in a position to assert that it has. Our judgment should be made with the modesty of those who are both judge and jury in their own cause.

Cycles of Progress and Decadence

(ii) (b) Turning from the evolution of the human being to the evolution of the human organization known as society, the principle of progress seems equally difficult to assert.

Each of the detailed arguments which are brought forward in support of the assertion of progress may be met with an equally reasonable denial. It is true that slaves have evolved into serfs, and serfs into free labourers. But many critics of the modern industrial system would contend that the lot of the worker under the capitalist order, who though theoretically free spends his life in bondage to the wages through which alone he can live, and in slavery to a machine which robs his work alike of the joy of creation and of the variety which lightened the toil of his ancestors, is in no way superior in leisure, dignity, or happiness to the state of the serfs of the Middle Ages or even of the slaves of the Classical world. An examination of such a book as "The Town Labourer," by J. L. Hammond and Barbara Hammond, would suggest to many that it was definitely inferior, and when it is remembered that the workers form numerically something like four-fifths of the society for which progress is claimed, the claim requires more confirmation than it has hitherto received.

The abuses of the industrial system which the passing of the Factory Acts has mitigated without abolishing, have seemed to many as grave a condemnation of the society which countenances them as the constant resort to violence and general insecurity which characterized the societies of the Middle Ages; and it is difficult to see that the lot of

INTUITIONISM AND THE MORAL SENSE

the miner who spends his days under the earth, or the lift boy who spends them in a lift, is much superior to that of the galley slave who spent them in the hold of a ship.

Similarly it is in all probability true that the change which substituted the morality of the Sermon on the Mount for the code of Deuteronomy, was a progressive development as well as a change. But the failure of the world to observe in practice any of the precepts of the Sermon on the Mount is notorious, and affords a standing example of the inability of society to make any progress over a period of two thousand years in the way of living up to a code of ethics which remains to-day as much of an unattainable, though not an impracticable ideal, as it was on the day it was promulgated.

In general it may be remarked that decadence no less than progress is a constant attribute of human societies.

The normal evolution of society is an evolution in which a period of progress precedes a period of decadence. No phenomenon in history is more remarkable than the apparent inability of human society to develop beyond a certain point. Egypt, Assyria, Chaldea, Babylon, Greece, Parthia and Rome, all declined in their turn. The close of the Classical era was followed by the Dark Ages which set the clock of progress back by some two thousand years, and left the work of civilizing the world to be begun over again. The recent war would suggest to some the beginning of a repetition of this process.

If therefore we are to assert any principle with regard to the development of society, it will be the principle of cycles rather than that of progress.

It is not established that progress in human society is continuous: it appears to persist for a varying period only, to be followed by a period of decadence which carries the swing of the world's pendulum back to the point at which it started.

Vagueness of Conception of Progress

(ii) (c) It will doubtless have already occurred to the reader that the whole of the question at issue turns upon the meaning given to the word progress.

If, for instance, we accept as our definition of progress Herbert Spencer's account of evolution as a process whereby " an indefinite, incoherent homogeneity is transformed into a definite, coherent heterogeneity," then the arguments which assert progress for the development of the individual and of society are valid. Evolution does in fact involve such a development, but that is no reason for identifying the development with our definition of progress. Half a dozen equally good formulæ could be given for the process of evolution, and each formula might with equal reason be defined as progress. The difficulty in defining progress arises, as Mr. Chesterton has pointed out, from the fact that the term implies not only change but direction, and direction involves a goal. If a man is walking along Whitehall between Trafalgar Square and the House of Commons, the process is quite clearly one involving change and motion. Equally clearly, however, it cannot be said to involve progress unless it is known at which end of Whitehall he desires to arrive. If he wishes to arrive at Trafalgar Square and is walking north, his motion is clearly a progress: if, however, he is walking south, it is not progress but retrogression.

Our definition of progress then depends upon our conception of the goal. But it is precisely with regard to this conception that the widest diversity of opinion exists.

"Whether," says Mr. Chesterton, "the future excellence lies in more law or less law, in more liberty or less liberty; whether property will be finally concentrated or finally cut up; whether sexual passion will reach its sanest in an almost virgin intellectualism, or in a full animal freedom; whether we should love everybody with Tolstoy or spare nobody with Nietzsche;—these are the things about which we are actually fighting most."

You cannot in fact assert progress for the development of the world unless you can indicate your goal. You cannot indicate your goal unless you have decided what things are good and valuable. To decide what things are good and valuable is one of the main objects of Ethics, and according to the theory which we have been considering it is one of the functions of the moral sense to make the decision. We cannot therefore hope to legitimize the moral sense by invoking the principle of progress, if we are compelled at the same time to establish a meaning for progress by appealing to the moral sense. The point is important since the theory we have been considering

INTUITIONISM AND THE MORAL SENSE

regards the principle of progress as the best means of establishing the validity of the various and changing deliverances of the moral sense; but we cannot make the moral sense depend upon progress, if progress in its turn depends upon the moral sense; each cannot be the basis of the other.

The arguments set out above are not intended to deny progress: they are only concerned to deny that it can be asserted, and for my own part I do not see how it is possible either to deny or to assert it. If this position is a sound one it is clear that the attempt to establish the evolution of the moral standard, on the ground that the societies, laws, and observances which the moral sense by its approval helps to maintain, themselves exhibit a principle of progress, cannot be substantiated.

From this it follows again that we have failed to arrive at any expedient for legitimizing the promptings of the moral sense. Until they can be so legitimized they must be regarded as in a measure irresponsible, and as such they clearly provide an inadequate criterion of right and wrong.

I will now proceed to consider the fifth and last argument which I wish to bring forward against the moral sense theories.

Nature of the Moral Sense

5. What is the nature and status of the moral sense? Is it some kind of feeling or emotion? Is it a kind of glorified instinct? Is it intuition which is usually regarded as a sort of amalgam of instinct and reason? Or is it purely rational?

Each of these views with regard to the nature of the moral sense has been held by philosophers, and as the binding force and the obligatory character of the deliverances of the moral sense depend upon the view we adopt, the question is one of considerable importance.

The Moral Sense as Feeling.

(i) Let us first consider the view that the moral sense is some kind of feeling.

There are two main grounds for this view:

How Primitive Feelings Evolve.

(i) (*a*) Many of the observances and requirements of morality seem to be the historical developments of what are undoubtedly primitive feelings in animals and savages.

When a dog obtains a bone, carries it away for secret consumption, and having satisfied himself with enough pickings for the moment, hides it carefully and strenuously resents any attempt on the part of others to exhume it or otherwise disturb his possession, he is exhibiting the germ of that feeling which lies at the basis of the sanctity of private property, which in its turn is the ground for the moral disapproval of stealing.

Just as naturalistic writers will show that fear is at the bottom of our religious sense, so will they prove with copious illustrations from the behaviour of primitive peoples that the possessive instinct, whether for property or women, is at the bottom of our moral sense, expressing itself in the highly organized moral code which disapproves of stealing and violence with regard to property, and inchastity, polygamy and violence with regard to women.

It is indeed significant that law, which is a man-made invention, is more severe on immorality in women than in men, and the inference may be drawn that, by means of the penalties it prescribes, and by the equally potent influence of the social taboo, men first endeavour to safeguard their right of ownership in women, and then proceed by a natural tendency of human nature to make a virtue of their feelings, and to call them moral because they happen to possess them. Whenever anything, however fantastic, is imposed on men whether by the needs of their own nature like sexual intercourse, or by outside forces like the necessity for clothes, they straightway make a virtue of it, and idealize it under sanctified appellations such as marriage in the one case, and decency in the other. Thus writers in the naturalistic strain!

Others trace the growth of the moral feeling to the social sense which is a fundamental human attribute.

Morality of its very nature implies more than one person. You cannot be moral all by yourself, and if human beings existed in solitude each on an isolated island the moral sense would not exist. But man has always lived in society. He is fundamentally gregarious. Morality is therefore a development of the feeling of sympathy which is a *sine quâ non* of the possibility of there being social life in a group.

Hence we tend to call moral whatever conduces to the interests of our group, and the feeling of group-solidarity is the basis of our so-called moral disapproval of actions like theft or violence which threaten the well-being of society.

If we accept Schopenhauer's definition of human society as " a collection of hedgehogs driven together for the sake of warmth," it is the moral sense which puts the felt upon the spikes.

Subjectivity and Objectivity

(i) (b) A familiar theory of perception, the theory of the philosophers, known as Empiricists, tells us that all knowledge is derived from sensation, and that *à priori* knowledge, that is knowledge which is acquired independently of the senses, is impossible.

From this it follows that our knowledge of what is right and wrong in common with our other knowledge is based on sensation and feeling. It is therefore conditioned by and dependent upon the nature of the feelings upon which it is based. Even if it may become something other than feeling it always retains something of the nature of its source; the feeling element dogs all its deliverances. Just as warmth is not in the fire but is a feeling produced in you by the fire, so immorality is not an attribute of actions but a characteristic of the sense which condemns them.

From these and similar considerations arises the theory that the moral sense is some kind of feeling.

Now it is important to note that if this view is taken the deliverances of the moral sense are robbed of all validity. The moral sense is in fact reduced to the level of feelings of taste.

If one man likes méringues and another dislikes them, the judgment of each is equally valid in the sense that it is a correct account of his own feelings. But this judgment of like or dislike is not a judgment about the méringues: it is a judgment about the feeling produced by them.

Similarly if morality is a kind of feeling, the statement that the action A is good and the action B is bad is not a statement about the qualities of the action A and the action B, but about the effect produced by the contemplation of those actions upon the speaker.

Moral judgments are therefore on this view judgments about the feelings of the person who makes them, and not judgments about conduct. In so far as the person who makes the judgment does possess the feelings, all moral judgments are equally valid. They are equally valid as judgments that those particular feelings are being entertained. In so far, however, as they purport to be more than that, in so far as they profess to say that the action A really is bad in itself because I have the feeling that it is bad, they possess no validity whatever. Furthermore, inasmuch as the contemplation of the action A may produce an entirely different feeling in some other person, a feeling namely that A is good, his judgment that A is good will be perfectly valid as an account of the feelings produced in him by A, although it will not be valid as an account of the real quality of A. If therefore the statement that A is good, or the statement that A is bad, means simply that some person entertains a particular feeling towards A, and means no more than that, and seeing that different persons may at the same time entertain feelings of a contrary character with regard to A, it is clearly possible for A to be both good and bad at the same time.

This is what is meant by the statement which is frequently made that morality is *subjective* only, and it is perfectly true that if the moral sense is a kind of feeling, morality cannot be more than purely subjective.

The use of the word subjective as applied to judgments of a moral sense, which is regarded as being a kind of feeling, is important and requires further explanation.

The difference between subjectivity and objectivity is a question of metaphysics and raises highly controversial issues. Many philosophers would deny that there is such a thing as objectivity at all.

In order to explain the sense in which I am using these terms, I propose to give one or two simple illustrations of a difference which in practice we all recognize, leaving the metaphysical questions (underlying the difference which I am assuming) to remain a bone of contention among metaphysicians.

To return to the case of méringues, when I say " méringues are palatable " my judgment may be termed

INTUITIONISM AND THE MORAL SENSE

subjective. What is meant is that the judgment is made not about the méringues but about the effect of the méringues on myself, the subject making the judgment. It is to be noted that the judgment " méringues are not palatable " is equally valid as being a correct account of the effect of the méringues on somebody else. There is, however, on objective fact, namely the actual palatableness of méringues, by reference to which one judgment can be shown to be more true or less true than the other.

To take an instance of another kind ; it is a well-known fact that railway lines appear to approach one another and ultimately to coincide as the distance from the eye increases. The judgment that they approach is again a case of a subjective judgment, being a judgment about the effect produced by the railway lines on the subject judging. In the case of the railway lines, however, it is known that they are equidistant, and this equidistance is regarded as an objective fact. The statement therefore that railway lines converge is a statement about the impression they create in the observer ; the statement that they are equidistant is a statement about the railway lines. The equidistance of the railway lines being regarded as an objective fact, provides a standard or criterion by which to convict of error the feeling of their convergence.

No such standard exists in the case of the méringues, and it is in this difference, the difference constituted by the presence or absence of an external standard, that the distinction between subjectivity and objectivity partly consists.

Now if the moral sense is regarded as a feeling only, it is clear that its deliverances may be regarded as parallel to our views about méringues. The statement " this action is immoral " becomes a statement not about the action but about somebody's feelings about the action ; as an account of those feelings it is correct, but as an account of the nature of the action it is no more correct than the contrary statement which affirms that the action is moral.

In the case of the railway lines there was always an objective fact, namely the equidistance of the lines, by reference to which the judgment that they converged could be convicted of error, and the judgment that they remained equidistant shown to be correct. But on the view which identifies moral sense with feeling there is no objective fact, namely the intrinsic goodness or badness of any particular action, by reference to which deliverances of the moral sense can be shown to be right or wrong.

Even if we were to assume for the sake of argument that an action had an intrinsic goodness or badness in its own right, we cannot know which kind of action it is, for since all judgments passed by the moral sense are judgments not about the action but about the feelings it excites, we can never know anything about the real nature of the action itself: we can never know therefore whether it is good or bad: and we can never know which of two varying judgments is the more correct.

If therefore the moral sense is some kind of feeling, all its deliverances are equally accurate; and none of them can be substantiated or verified. The conventional moralist who believes stealing to be wrong can have no ground for reproaching the burglar, who in the act of appropriating his spoons bluntly asserts that wealth being at present unevenly distributed, any attempt by private individuals to readjust the balance has the complete approval of his moral sense; and maintains that prisons and the penal code which assert that some actions are crimes which society is justified in punishing are monuments of arbitrary irrationality.

A moral action becomes in this view simply an action which is approved by the moral feelings of the majority of people. In Hume's words, "Actions are not approved because they are moral: they are moral because they are approved."

It is clear therefore that any attempt to identify the moral sense with feeling not only cuts at the objective basis of all morality, but by asserting that moral conduct is simply that which happens to obtain the approval of the majority at any given moment, nullifies the teaching of history, which shows that any advance in the current standard of morality invariably comes from the insight and understanding of a few individuals, who are roundly abused for immorality by the majority because they dare to question the propriety of what the majority approves.

If morality is conduct which is approved by most people

INTUITIONISM AND THE MORAL SENSE

at the time, Christ was obviously one of the most immoral characters recorded in history.

The Moral Sense as Instinct

(ii) An attempt is sometimes made to escape this repellent conclusion by identifying the moral sense not with some kind of feeling, but with some form of instinct. There is a tendency to regard instinct as something unique and infallible. Instincts, it is argued, are not arbitrary, they do not arise out of nothing, and they must be significant of something: the fact that they are experienced is therefore regarded as a sufficient ground for trusting them.

Writers with an evolutionary tendency are inclined to make much of this point. The instinct that prompts the squirrel to store nuts is salutary because the winter is coming: the instinct which prompts the hedgehog to roll itself into a ball is salutary because danger is imminent: the instinct which makes the savage forebode evil when thunder is in the air is salutary because lightning is dangerous; therefore it is argued that the instinct which makes us approve of certain actions as moral is salutary, and may be trusted implicitly, although it is unable to give an account of itself. The old woman who tells you, " Right is right and wrong is wrong, and a' can allus tell one from t'other," is an exponent of this view. The fact that the moral instinct is possessed, is in fact regarded as sufficient evidence of its trustworthiness.

The defects of this view are obvious.

Instincts, whatever be their source, are as frequently fallacious as trustworthy. If a hen is put to sit on ducks' eggs, she will have an instinct when the ducklings are hatched to prevent them from entering the water: but the fact that she possesses the instinct does not mean that the instinct is trustworthy, nor that it is dangerous for the ducklings to enter the water. Animals have an instinct to seek the woods when thunder is in the air, and human beings with colds have an instinct for stuffy rooms.

Furthermore the supporters of the instinct view will not agree that we should trust all our instincts. They are usually uncompromising moralists who would regard with horror any suggestion that we should give free play to the sexual instinct, and roundly denounce as immoral a philosophy such as that of Walter Pater or of Oscar Wilde which urges the indulgence of instinct for its own sake or in the interests of experience.

By what principle then do supporters of this school distinguish evil instincts which are not to be trusted, from the moral instinct which is to be implicitly obeyed?

The answer is of course by the principle of reason. Reason is invoked to discriminate between a beneficial instinct and a harmful instinct. It is reason which legitimizes the promptings of the one and represses those of the other. It is by an appeal to reason alone that the advocate of the moral sense view can find any ground for deprecating the promiscuous indulgence of the sexual instinct, while advocating the promiscuous indulgence of the moral instinct.

The Moral Sense as Reason

(iii) This brings us to a consideration of the third and chief alternative view as to the nature of the moral sense, the view that it is rational; for, once the intrusion of reason is admitted, there is no longer anything to be gained by maintaining that our moral judgments are compounded of instinct or feeling only. Although we may grant that there is a strong admixture of feeling in every moral judgment, it is a feeling which is guided and informed by reason. A feeling of moral approval or moral repulsion is doubtless at the bottom of every such judgment: without it it would be impossible to explain how the judgment came to be passed, but it is a feeling which requires reason to justify and legitimize its expression. Feeling is the steam which sets the engine of our moral machinery going, but the direction which the engine takes is determined by reason which plays the part of the driver who holds the levers. Once, however, the fact that our moral judgments are rational is granted, it becomes clear that they cannot be divorced from a consideration of consequences.

It is not rational to pass moral judgments on actions in themselves, on the ground that they are either good or bad in their own right apart from the consequences they produce, and it is only by divesting the moral sense of any admixture of reason that we can suppose that moral judgments are passed in this way.

INTUITIONISM AND THE MORAL SENSE

Reason demands that the consequences of actions should be taken into account. They must be taken into account because we have seen that an action only is what it is, when considered in conjunction with its consequences; that without them it is featureless, being deprived of those characteristics in virtue of which it is judged good or bad.

Actions and their consequences form an indivisible whole, no part of which can form the subject of a judgment of value independently of its relation to the other parts; and as it is irrational to pass judgment on a whole, when you are only acquainted with the part, it is imperative that we should take consequences into account if we are to regard moral judgments as something other than purely instinctive feelings of liking and disliking.

Consequences are objective concrete facts. As such they provide us with an objective standard whereby to estimate the value of actions and to correct the deliverances of the moral sense, just as the equidistance of the railway lines provided a standard for the correction of the judgment that they converged.

By admitting the importance of consequences, we elevate judgments of right and wrong out of the region of subjectivity which is the sphere of disputes as to the palatableness of méringues, and arrive at a definite standard which will serve as our criterion of right and wrong.

Summary of Moral Sense Theories and Criticisms

We have now concluded our survey of the arguments which can be brought against the moral sense theory in any of the various forms in which it has been maintained. If these arguments are correct, we cannot hold that the rightness or wrongness of actions or classes of actions consists in any unique and intrinsic characteristic attaching to certain actions or classes of actions in their own right; nor that it depends upon the motive from which they are performed; nor upon the consequences which it is intended that the actions should produce, as opposed to the consequences which they do in fact produce; nor upon any deliverances of the moral sense or senses of any persons or body of persons with regard to the actions in question.

For the purpose of convenience we may summarize the

various forms under which the moral sense theory is held as follows.

The moral sense theories regard the rightness or wrongness of actions as dependent upon the opinions entertained towards them by certain persons or bodies of persons. The theories which emphasize the importance of motive or free will or intended consequences, regard the opinion entertained towards his actions by the agent himself as being the criterion; theories which emphasize the social character of the moral sense, or the moral uniqueness of certain classes of actions, look for their criterion to the opinion entertained about these actions not by the agent but by the body of persons called the community.

In all these forms, the moral sense theory appears to be open to such serious objections that it becomes necessary to look elsewhere for our criterion of right and wrong. If therefore we take the view that the rightness or wrongness of actions is not determined by the opinions or feelings of any person or body of persons, we arrive by process of elimination at the theory described in our first chapter which makes rightness and wrongness depend upon the nature of the actual consequences produced.

We have seen that this theory regarded as valuable only those consequences which consisted of the maximum possible quantity of pleasure or happiness; and we have now to consider the question which was left unexamined in the first chapter, namely whether pleasure is the only element of which we are to take account in estimating the nature of the consequences of an action.

§ 3. WHAT CONSEQUENCES ARE VALUABLE?

The theory which was considered in the first chapter defined a right action as that which produced the best consequences on the whole. To determine what is meant by the best consequences, it is clear that we must arrive at some conception of what is good.

Reasons were given in the first chapter for regarding pleasure as a good: we also saw that there were reasons for not regarding it as the only good. We have therefore to ask what is good besides pleasure?

The question of what is good, or rather what is The Good, used to be the central problem of Ethics. Philosophers in Classical times used to go about looking for The Good as though it were a kind of hidden treasure, much as in the Middle Ages they devoted their lives to the quest of the Philosopher's Stone, or the Elixir of Life. The view was commonly held that only one thing was good, and that for the sake of this one thing everything else was desired. The Good was supremely valuable, and was desired for its own sake: other things were valuable only in so far as they tended to bring us nearer to The Good. The difficulty of this view lay in the impossibility of agreeing upon a satisfactory definition of what The Good was; it has been variously identified with Pleasure, Truth, Virtue, Beauty, Knowledge, and Intellectual Contemplation, and volumes have been written by the supporters of each of these conceptions to prove that their particular good was ultimate, and that other apparent goods were only regarded as such because they conduced to The Good.

On this subject we have surprisingly little to say. The fundamental problem of Ethics has ceased to be fundamental, simply because the notion of "The One Good" has had to be abandoned. The view is now generally taken that instead of there being one ultimate good there are several, several different things that is, each of which is desired for its own sake, and in order to discover what these things are, we have simply to answer the question: "What is in fact desired?"

Before giving the reasons for this view, I want to make three preliminary observations which will have the effect of clearing the issue.

The Good is Indefinable

(i) Ultimate goods are indefinable. By an ultimate good is meant that which is desired for its own sake, and not for the sake of something else.

The distinction involved between ultimate goods and other kinds of goods, goods that is which are good for a particular purpose, is an obvious one. Let us assume for moment that health is an ultimate good. If a man has cold he is told that quinine is good for him, and he accordingly desires to obtain quinine. It is clear that he does not desire quinine for its own sake; it is also clear that although he is told that quinine is good for him, he does not regard quinine as a good in itself. He only desires quinine because he believes that it may banish his cold and restore him to health, and he regards quinine therefore as good for this particular purpose. Quinine is a good, therefore, because it conduces to health, and its value is derived from the end which it promotes.

Now if health is an ultimate good, it is ultimate in the sense that it is not desired, as quinine is desired, for the sake of anything else. Its value cannot therefore be expressed in terms of any other form of value, as the value of quinine can be expressed in terms of its conduciveness to health. If health is an ultimate good, therefore, its value, or that in virtue of which it is good, is unique.

Now all definition consists in describing one thing in terms of something else. This is true both of correct and incorrect definitions. If, for instance, we consider Samuel Butler's definition of faith as the " power of believing in things which are known to be untrue," the definition depends for the fact of its being made and understood on the possibility of expressing faith in terms of belief. Faith is regarded and spoken of as a certain kind of belief : it is not something unique. Similarly the definition of a regular pentagon as a " figure bounded by five equal straight lines " depends upon the possibility of the peculiar attributes of a pentagon being expressed in terms of equality and of straight lines.

Ultimate things, however, just because they are unique, cannot be expressed in terms of something else. We may define faith in terms of belief, and belief in terms of something else, knowledge for instance, but in the long run we must always arrive at something which, owing to the uniqueness of its characteristics, cannot be defined in terms of anything else.

Ultimate goods are of this character.

The Good Desired Irrationally

(ii) Good is the object of desire, not of reason.

Desire sets the end of our actions : reason plans the necessary steps for the achievement of that end.

As a rule the ends we place before ourselves in action are only desired for the sake of something else. A boy desires success in an examination because it will bring a diploma or degree. He desires a diploma because it will

INTUITIONISM AND THE MORAL SENSE 61

assist him to gain a situation. He desires a situation because it will bring him money. He desires money at first because it will bring enjoyment or security: later he desires money for its own sake. But the ultimate thing, for the sake of which other things are desired, is as much an object of desire as the succession of achievements which bring it nearer.

It is true that we may reason about our desires, and endeavour to interpret them to ourselves. Reason may also control or repress desires; but when it does so it is only in the interest of something else which reason believes to be the object of a stronger desire, as when a man represses his desire to smoke before a Rugby football match in the interests of his stronger desire to keep his wind during the match. But reason plays no part in determining what we desire.

Many of our desires have been shown by psycho-analysts to be unconscious desires. Unconscious desires cannot properly be said to have any end or object in view; certainly they have no end which has been set by reason.

An Intuitionism of Ends

(iii) If ultimate goods are objects of desire, it is absurd to ask why they are desired! It is impossible to give reasons for our desires for ultimates. The only reason that can be given for the desire for an object is that it is desired for the sake of some other object. Objects which are not desired for this reason are desired for no reason at all.

No answer can be given to the question, why we desire health or appreciate beauty: nor can we say why we find music pleasing. It is of course possible to identify elements in, and reasons for, the appreciation of a particular piece of music, or the work of a particular composer: we may be attracted by the brilliancy of a pianist's execution, by the greatness of a composer's conception, by the spirit and vivacity which animates a particular piece, or by the sentimental reminiscences that it arouses in ourselves. These, however, are not reasons for our liking music generally: they are reasons for our admiration of a particular piece. Of music generally we can say no more than that it pleases us, because we are made like that.

Ultimate goods then are indefinable and unanalyzable.

They are the objects of desires of which no account can be given except that we have them. They are desired, that is, irrationally and instinctively.

If follows therefore that if we wish to know what are the ultimate goods, what are the valuable things by a reference to which we can estimate the " best consequences of an action," we have only to look into our hearts to find out what things are actually desired for their own sake. The question becomes a question of psychology.

Easy as it appears at first sight, however, this is a remarkably difficult performance. Apart from the fact that many of our desires are unconscious and that many of our conscious desires are delusive, being really desires for something other than they profess,[1] it is very difficult to distinguish desires which are desires for things which are valuable for their own sake, from those which are desires for things valued for the sake of something else. We have seen that many philosophers have maintained that only pleasure is desired for its own sake and that all other things are desired for the sake of pleasure. Although we have cited reasons for regarding this psychology as false, it is by no means easy to specify what things are desired for their own sake besides pleasure.

One of the reasons for this difficulty is that different people probably desire different things for their own sake.

It is considerations of this kind which lie at the basis of what is known as the new Intuitionism, popularized by Dr. G. E. Moore.

We have seen reasons for regarding the old Intuitionism, which held that the moral sense provided us with unique feelings or intuitions with regard to right and wrong actions, as unsatisfactory largely because feeling was not an adequate or trustworthy criterion of morality. It was not adequate because it relied upon the help of reason to legitimize itself among all the other feelings as the one feeling which ought to be trusted, and to discredit the indulgence of other feelings. So soon as reason was invoked in the process, it proclaimed that actions must be judged by their consequences.

Intuitions about conduct are therefore unsatisfactory.

[1] The phenomena of unconscious and delusive desires will be dealt with at greater length in Chapter V.

An Intuition which says, "This is right," must give an account of itself before the bar of reason, which is the only faculty in a position to provide adequate or at least plausible grounds for the distinction between right and wrong.

But with regard to goods the case is different. We have seen that reason plays no part in setting our ends, and that our desires cannot therefore be expected to provide rational grounds for themselves.

Here then is a more legitimate field for Intuition.

We can and do have Intuitions as to what is good, which cannot be corrected by reason or expected to give a rational account of themselves, simply because desire for the good is not a rational process. Intuitions which tell us, "This is good," are probably the best if not the only means at our disposal of discovering what are those goods which are desired for their own sake; and these Intuitions tell us that virtue, knowledge, beauty, pleasure, intellectual and bodily activity are all so desired.

But this does not mean that they are desired in isolation as if they were static, self-existent, independent entities. The best consequences are not those which contain a certain fixed percentage of truth, plus a certain fixed percentage of pleasure, plus a certain fixed percentage of virtue, and so on. What is meant is that truth, pleasure, virtue and the rest, each constitute an element of ultimate value, which must be taken into account in making our estimate of what consequences are the best. Those consequences which contain the greatest proportion of any or all of these elements of value will be the best consequences, just as those lives will be the best which contain the greatest proportion of these same elements.

But people being differently constituted, will desire different things, or different quantities of the same thing, so that the proportions in which these elements of value will be arranged will vary from person to person, the most desirable proportion for each person being fixed by yet another intuition or judgment of value on the part of the person concerned.

Good therefore is not a fixed unit. It is a collection of heterogeneous elements each of which is good in itself, in so far as it is desired for its own sake. One man's good is different from another man's, and good will change for the same man, as the proportions in which the various elements of value are arranged change, as the results of changes of desire.

Results of Examination of Utilitarianism and Intuitionism

In this and the first chapter I have considered two main groups of ethical theories: the Utilitarian group which looks for the criterion of rightness and wrongness to the consequences of actions, and the Intuitionist or moral sense group which looks to the judgments of the moral sense.

As a result of the examination of these theories we are in a position to enunciate the following propositions:

1. The rightness or wrongness of actions does not depend upon the feelings or opinions of any person or body of persons with regard to those actions, whether those feelings or opinions take the form of the emanations of a free will, or of a moral motive on the part of the agent, or of a unique sentiment of approval or disapproval with regard to certain actions or classes of actions, which are themselves regarded as unique.

2. Rightness or wrongness does depend upon actual consequences, those actions being right which have the best consequences on the whole.

This proposition remains true, although it is not humanly possible to estimate the total consequences of any action, and not therefore possible ever to judge of any action that it is absolutely right.

3. In estimating the value of consequences with a view to ascertaining what are the best, several elements of value, each of which constitutes an object of desire for its own sake, must be admitted.

4. Pleasure is not the only element of ultimate value, although no mental whole is valuable without a certain admixture of pleasure.

5. Elements of value are established by intuitions which formulate our goods for us. These intuitions are intuitions with regard to the goodness of ends, and not with regard to the rightness of conduct. These intuitions also determine the various proportions in which elements of value should be combined to constitute the best life for each individual.

6. The best life for each individual is not constant, but varies according to variations in individual desire.

CHAPTER III

THE FORM OF THE GOOD

NO survey of leading Ethical theories would be complete without some account of Plato's doctrine of the Form of the Good. It is not a view which numbers many adherents to-day, but it gives nevertheless a very attractive and plausible explanation of what is meant by calling an action good, and is very difficult if not impossible to disprove.

In order to avoid confusion it will be convenient to use a specific epithet to describe the ethical value of actions judged by Plato's standard, as I have already done in the case of actions judged by the Utilitarian and Intuitionist standards. Actions judged by the Utilitarian standard of the consequences they produced, I have called right and wrong; actions judged by the Intuitionist standard of the deliverances of the moral sense, moral and immoral; actions judged in accordance with Plato's doctrine of the Form of Good, will be called good and bad.

I do not mean by this distinction to imply that a good action is necessarily different from a moral action or from a right action: they are frequently the same; nor do I mean to suggest that there can be two equally true criteria of right and wrong. The distinction is only adopted provisionally for the purposes of discussion, so that in speaking of a good action I may be understood to mean an action which would be regarded as good on Plato's theory, without necessarily saying so every time the words are used.

§ 1. STATEMENT OF PLATO'S THEORY

Plato's theory of the Form of Good cannot be treated independently of his general theory of Forms of which a brief account must be given.

The theory is primarily a logical one, and raises logical

and metaphysical questions of a most controversial character. It will not be possible to enter into a discussion of these questions in a book which is concerned only with Ethics; but some of them will be briefly indicated in so far as they constitute objections to the ethical criterion which the theory sets up. The theory falls into two parts which will be considered separately.

What the Forms are

1. Plato's theory starts from the consideration of such a conception as "whiteness." In endeavouring to discover what whiteness is, he proceeds to consider a number of white objects with a view to discovering what they have in common. Whatever differences a number of white objects may present they all possess a common quality, namely the quality of being white. This quality of being white or whiteness is not any one of the objects which possess it; nor is it their sum, for if all the white objects that existed in the universe were collected together they would not constitute whiteness, but simply the sum total of white objects. Whiteness then is something other than the various objects which are white. Not only is it something other than these objects, but it exists in its own right apart from them. Whiteness by itself is clearly something, for we cannot entertain a thought about nothing, and the word does have a meaning for us, which enables us to think of it. If whiteness were nothing, a thought about whiteness would be the same as a thought about blackness, or about redness; the fact that a thought about whiteness is different from a thought about redness, shows both that whiteness exists to be thought about, and that it possesses qualities which distinguish it from redness.

Now while the many things which are white are different, the whiteness in virtue of which we call them white is always one and always the same. White things may change, becoming white at one time and ceasing to be white at another, but whiteness remains unaffected by these changes and is eternally identical with itself.

For reasons into which we need not now enter, Plato regarded the world with which we are in touch by means of our senses, the world of changing white objects, as an unreal

THE FORM OF THE GOOD

world. It is different at different moments; and different for different people. What is blue for one man is grey for his colour-blind brother, and unless we are slavishly to accept the judgment of the majority as a criterion of truth, there is no more reason for asserting that it is really blue than that it is really grey.

With regard to such a world it is not possible to possess exact knowledge, we can entertain opinions about it only.

The real world must be a world of which it is possible to have exact knowledge: it must therefore be static and unchangeable; it is in fact a world composed of just those conceptions, such as whiteness, which have been seen to remain one and unchanging, while white objects change at different times and for different people.

Plato held that such a world did in fact exist; that as opposed to the world of objects which are known by means of the senses, it is known by reason only, and that the entities which compose it are the cause of the existence of objects like white posts, and white cream, which appear to be real because they are known to the senses, but are in fact only half real.

Conceptions such as whiteness Plato calls the Form of whiteness. White objects he speaks of as particulars which partake of the Form of whiteness. Cream, the conduct of Christ, and the triangle A B C, are particulars of the Forms of whiteness, goodness and triangularity, whiteness, goodness and triangularity being always something other than the particular instances of them with which we are acquainted.

For Plato there exists a Form for every group of objects which have a common quality, and it is because of their participation in the Form that the objects exhibit the characteristics they appear to possess. Thus a table is round and smooth by virtue of its participation in the Forms of roundness and smoothness. It is not round and smooth in its own right.

While the Forms are perfect and complete, the objects which participate in them are only imperfect representations or manifestations of the Forms. Plato speaks of objects as approximating to the nature of the Forms, and trying as it were to be more perfect embodiments of the Forms in which they participate. It may be asked how, if we can never know the Forms completely, but only know the particulars or objects in which they are imperfectly manifest, we can know that the Forms exist, or recognize their manifestation when we see it?

Plato answers this question with the doctrine of metempsychosis or the transmigration of souls.

The soul, which is immortal, is from time to time embodied in a corporeal form for life upon the earth. During the period intervening between any two such lives the soul sojourns in a heavenly place, wherein she is in constant and complete communion with the Forms, which are there completely manifested, instead of being dimly apprehended through the distorting medium of physical objects. When the soul returns to earth encased in her bodily prison, the faint remembrance which she has of her vision of the Forms enables her to recognize their manifestation in the various objects of which the body is aware by means of the senses.

While perception of a white object then is in the first place due to the stimulation of the senses, the apprehension of its particular quality of whiteness is the work of the soul, and is in reality an act of recognition.

In the light of this doctrine we can now state the first part of Plato's theory of the good. A good act is one which partakes of the Form of goodness, and is recognized as such by the remembrance which the soul possesses of the Form of goodness which it has known in a previous state of existence.

A brief examination of some of the implications of this doctrine will reveal some of the objections to which it is open.

The Forms not Mental

(a) It has frequently been supposed by commentators on Plato that the Forms are intended to be some kind of mental entity. This supposition has been reinforced by the fact that the usual English name for the Greek word which I have translated as " Form " is " Idea." This view of the Forms is a complete travesty of Plato. It is indeed suggested by him in one of the Dialogues, but only to be promptly repudiated.

The Forms are non-mental entities, the objects of thought, but not in any way the content or substance of thought. They are not thought by any mind, in the sense that they

THE FORM OF THE GOOD

are ideas or thoughts in that mind : they are thought of as something existing apart from mind.

It follows that their existence is completely independent of the physical world. They exist separate and apart, eternal and immutable entities. They are the patterns on the model of which God created the world, existing before the world, and independently of God.

Relations between Forms and Particulars

(b) The relation between the Form and the series of particulars which partake of it, is sometimes spoken of as one in which the Form is the cause of the existence of the particulars, sometimes as one in which the particulars are created on the model of, or in the likeness of the Form, but owe their existence to some other source. Either view leads to difficulties.

As a result of the implications considered in (a) above, we have to suppose that the world of Forms is one which is different in substance and reality from the world we know by means of the senses ; it exists neither in time nor in space ; if therefore the world of physical objects were swept into oblivion and all human consciousness perished with it, the world of Forms would remain unaffected.

If this is a true account of the Forms, it is argued that the nature of their being must be so different from that of objects of sense, that the Forms cannot enter into any relation with such objects, much less be their innermost essence, the cause of their being endowed with such reality as they have.

Yet if the particular is a mere copy of the Form, that part of the theory which ascribes the possession of any quality, such as whiteness, by any object, such as cream to the presence of a Form in the object, falls to the ground.

Our Knowledge of the World of Forms

(c) These difficulties are not altogether insoluble, although an attempt to reconcile them would t ke us far from our present theme. It must be admitted, however, that the theory gets into difficulties which border on the absurd, when it deals with physical objects of a mean and sordid character, such as hair and mud. It is difficult to believe in the existence of a transcendent Form of hair, or of a chimerical entity such as a purple quadratic equation, which we may choose to invent for the purpose of postulating a Form to endow it with the peculiar combination of qualities in virtue of which it is what it is.

Although these difficulties are brought to light when all the implications of the theory are pushed to their logical conclusion, there is no doubt that with regard to certain spheres of knowledge, it provides as satisfactory an answer as has yet been given to that quest for objectivity which we have seen to be at the basis of most ethical inquiry.

These spheres are pre-eminently those of Ethics and Mathematics.

For Plato the physical world, as we have already noted, was incapable of being an object of accurate knowledge; simply because it could not be analyzed into those combinations of static logical concepts with which scientific knowledge was supposed to deal.

As scientific knowledge is possible, it must be knowledge of something other than this irrational physical world; therefore it deals with a world of entities which lie entirely beyond the range of any possible experience on the part of the senses.

In giving examples of the sort of scientific knowledge we possess of this world, Plato draws his illustrations mainly from two spheres, those of Mathematics and Ethics. Now Ethics was, for Plato, subject to the same laws as Mathematics, the qualities of order, measure and proportion being essential characteristics of the morally good. It follows therefore that the real world, including the real basis of morality, is a world of fixed entities, subject to mathematical laws and known with a precision which is applicable only to mathematical objects. Of the world of Forms then we have true knowledge : of the half-real world of sensible objects we have probable opinion only.

This distinction admirably suits the approximate and controversial character of ethical judgments.

Just as in mathematics the straight line we draw is not the straight line we reason about, or to which our conclusions apply, for it has breadth as well as length and is not entirely straight ; so in passing judgments upon human ethical actions, we never pass judgment upon what is purely

THE FORM OF THE GOOD

good, but upon an imperfect manifestation of it imperfectly recognized.

Because our ethical judgments are matters of opinion only, they differ at different times, and among different people at the same time. But the fact of their differences does not alter our unanimous conviction of the reality of the good itself, although we may never fully apprehend it. We all know that there is such a thing as morality, much as we may differ about its meaning and its significance.

The Unique Position of the Form of Good

2. Plato conceives of the Form of the Good in two different ways. The first conception is that which we have just described. The Form of the Good is regarded as one among a number of Forms, possessing greater reality and greater importance than the various particular acts in which it is manifested, but not more real or more important than the other Forms. It occupies no special or unique place in the hierarchy of reality, and the particulars in which it appears and of whose being it is the cause form a strictly limited class. According to this conception the Form of Good is regarded as tending to manifest itself more particularly in actions, while the Form of Beauty appears in physical objects, and the Form of Truth in judgments. It is true that there are passages where Plato speaks of objects or institutions as participating in the Good, but these are rare, and as a rule the Good is regarded as a purely ethical conception which is the source of such ethical value as actions possess. There is, however, a famous passage in the Republic in which the Form of Good is treated in a very different manner.

In this passage Plato is speaking of the function which Philosophy has to play in examining the axioms and hypotheses of the special sciences, as for instance the postulates which the geometrician takes for granted in his reasoning. By a process of rigidly testing and sifting these hypotheses, Philosophy reduces them to a still smaller group of ultimate hypotheses, from which they can and have been derived. This smaller group of hypotheses or ultimate principles will upon further examination be found to reduce itself to one which is the cause of such truth as the others possess and the ground from which they may be deduced. This ultimate principle is self-evidently true, and when it has once been perceived by the philosopher, he will proceed from it to deduce the real ultimate principles upon which the special sciences are founded, and to substitute these for the erroneous ultimates hitherto assumed as hypotheses by scientists.

The process may be compared to ascending a ladder by stepping upon the rungs of scientific hypotheses until the top is reached. The top is contiguous to the top of an adjoining ladder, which the former climber will then descend, manufacturing as he proceeds the rungs upon which he steps. It may also be noted that the process is closely akin to the speculations of modern mathematicians, such as Peano, who are inclined to regard the whole of mathematical science as a system of deductions from a few logical premises.

It is, however, a matter of some surprise to find that the all-important logical principle from which the hypothesis of the special sciences are derived is the Form of the Good. Just as each particular in the world of sensible objects is a manifestation or aspect of its own appropriate Form which is exhibited in it and is the source of its being, so the Forms themselves are regarded as stretching in an ordered sequence or hierarchy up to the Form of the Good, of which they in their turn are but aspects, and to which they owe the source of their being.

The Form of the Good has a twofold function. It is at once the cause of the existence of the other Forms, and through them of the objects of the world of sense, and also the cause of their being known. In this connection it is compared with the sun, which is at once the source of the warmth and heat which are the cause of growth and vitality in nature, and also of the light whereby the objects of nature are beheld.

The Form of Good is not beautiful or true, nor is it identical with the Forms of Beauty or Truth, but it is the source of both. All being and all existence may be regarded as emanations of the Form of Good, possessing an ever diminishing degree of reality, as their distance from the source of their being increases, so that we may i entify the Form of Good with what in another of the Dialogues Plato describes as the " Maker and Father of all."

Plato's description of the nature and functions of the Form of Good is generally clothed in such mystical language that it is difficult to grasp his meaning with any degree of precision. It is clear, however, that he meant to convey much more by the conception than a poetical faith that "God is in his heaven," and hence that "All is well with the world," or in other words, that the essence and purpose of the Universe is good.

Reduced so far as possible to logical statement the theory amounts to this: it is always possible to distinguish between two kinds of causes: the first is the true cause; the second may be described as the sum of the accessory conditions. Now the true cause cannot operate or become efficacious without the presence of the accessory conditions, which may themselves therefore be looked upon as being in a sense a kind of cause. The true cause of the existence of the world and of every arrangement and object in the world is the principle of the Form of Good which is that "It is best that things should be so." The accessory conditions for the creation of the world are found in the existence of the chaotic disorderly matter out of which the world is made, and through which the principle, "It is best that things should be so," strives to manifest itself. It is because of the disorderly material in which it has to work that the principle of good, though always present as the underlying factor in the arrangements of the world, is frequently obscured and overlaid, and hence arises the appearance of evil and imperfection in the world. The Forms, however, which possess no ingredient of matter in their structure, are pure embodiments of the principle of good.

Hence we may regard the second or more mystical treatment of the Form of Good as a statement of the doctrine that the fundamental structure of the universe is ethical in character, and that it is not only ethical but ethically good.

Although it may be a little fanciful to interpret the Form of Good, as one writer does, as "a rational, consistent conception of the greatest possible attainable human happiness, of the ultimate laws of God, nature or man that sanction conduct, and of the consistent operation of those laws in legislation, government, and education," there can be no doubt that it constitutes an assertion that the fundamental nature of things is neither mechanically neutral, nor purposively and spiritually benevolent, but consists of something which is strictly good although it is not necessarily good as the expression of any willing mind.

The refusal to identify the principle of good with a benevolent personal deity is important. The Form of Good is not to be confused with any conception of God. It may be regarded as that on the model of which God made the world, but it existed antecedently to God, and is known by God as something which is independent of Himself. But this latter conception is by no means certain, for Plato's language about God is always of a mystical and poetic character, and creating it is not certain that he definitely thought of God as the world. There are passages, it is true, which suggest such a conception, but the idea of God is in no way essential to Plato's system, the existence of the world as we know it being adequately accounted for by the manifestations of the world of Forms in sensible objects.

§ 2. Implications of the Theory

If we leave out of account the import of the more transcendent and mystical developments of the Form of Good, described above, the significance of the theory for Ethics may be briefly summarized as follows:

1. The theory differs from the Intuitionist and Utilitarian theories in a very important particular.

The Intuitionist theories held that the ethical value of an action depended upon some person or class of persons having a certain attitude with regard to it, namely an attitude of moral approval.

The Utilitarian theory held that the ethical value of an action depended upon its consequences, and that a right action was one which had the best consequences on the whole. Since, however, the total sum of the actual consequences of an action can never be known to any person but can only be guessed at, the theory states in effect that what is of importance in estimating the rightness or wrongness of an action is not the total consequences which remain unknown, but the attitude of some person or class of persons towards such consequences as are known. A right action is therefore, for practical purposes, one whose observed consequences are such as to excite an attitude of approval in the mind of the person judging.

Both groups of theories therefore have this in common, that their ethical judgments, which profess to be judgments about actions, are in fact judgments about people's attitude towards actions.

They never succeed in valuing the action itself: they always value people's opinions about it, or attitude towards it, and in so doing they make the ethical criterion of an action depend not on any intrinsic quality possessed by the action or by its consequences, but upon the quality of people's sentiments towards the action or its consequences.

As opposed to these theories Plato's doctrine of the Form of Good (I am here referring only to the first part of the doctrine) does succeed in formulating a criterion which applies directly to actions in themselves.

It states that the goodness or badness of an action does not depend upon its consequences, nor does it depend upon the opinions of any person or body of persons about it, but it does depend upon the extent to which it participates in the Form of Good.

Ethical judgments therefore on this theory are judgments with regard to the presence or absence of the Form of Good in the action under consideration.

2. Not only is the Form of Good manifested in different degrees in different actions, but people possess in different degrees the power of recognizing it.

Just as in art persons of good taste and of bad taste are persons who possess respectively different capacities for recognizing the Form of Beauty in objects, so a person with a highly developed moral standard is a person who possesses in a high degree the power of recognizing actions which participate in the Form of Good. A highly developed community with an elaborate code of morals is a community consisting largely of persons of this character; whereas a community which regards it as moral to roast persons whose opinions, though enlightened, are unpopular, has a low capacity for recognizing the absence of the Form of Good and the presence of the Form of Badness.

Progress therefore means growth in the power to recognize those actions in which the Form of Good is present.

3. As we never completely apprehend the Form itself

during our earthly existence, and as it is never completely apparent in any particular action, no moral judgment can be more than approximately correct, just as no action can be more than approximately good.

It is therefore never possible to say that such and such an action is absolutely good, any more than it is possible to predicate absolute certainty for one's belief that a certain action is good: it is possible, in Plato's words, to have "probable opinion only." But this does not mean that some actions are not better than others, nor does it mean that some people's moral judgments and moral codes are not better than the judgments and codes of others.

The fact that you cannot tell which of two conflicting moral judgments about an action is right, does not alter the fact that one is more nearly right than the other: and this remains true although it is not humanly possible to state with certainty which of the two judgments is in fact the one which is more nearly right. To take an analogy, we may assume that at the bottom of the Atlantic, exactly midway between Ireland and America, there is a rock which has never been seen by human eyes. Now it is clear that such a rock possesses a temperature of its own, although that temperature has never been measured. If two people make two different guesses at the temperature of this rock, it is clear that nobody will be able to tell which of the two guesses is more correct. That does not, however, alter the fact that one of the two guesses is in fact more correct than the other, although nobody can with certainty identify it.

But just as one guess at the temperature might be palpably absurd, while the other might be clearly approximately correct, so it is possible to say that of two conflicting estimates of the morality of an action, one is much more likely to be correct than the other; and it is possible to say this although an absolutely certain affirmation in the matter is impossible.

Advantages of Plato's Position

The advantages of Plato's theory are therefore fourfold:

1. It does provide for judgments about the value of actions themselves and not about people's attitude towards them.

THE FORM OF THE GOOD

2. It does provide an objective standard of goodness to which some actions can be said to approximate more than others, instead of regarding differences of morality as equivalent to subjective differences of taste.

3. It explains how it is that the opinions of different people and of different communities with regard to morality differ, showing such differences to be differences in the capacity for recognition.

4. It also provides a meaning for the conception of moral progress, and a practical, although not an absolute, standard by which to measure the respective values of different ethical codes.

Under all these heads the theory squares to a remarkable degree with the facts of morality as we know them, satisfying as it does that desire for objectivity and a standard, which we all instinctively feel to exist in morals, and at the same time reconciling the existence of such a standard with the notorious differences of moral judgments.

CHAPTER IV

SUMMARY OF ETHICAL THEORIES

§ 1. Reconciliation of Utilitarianism, Intuitionism and the Theory of Forms

IN the preceding three chapters I have considered three main groups of ethical theories. These theories may be said to be roughly representative of the great majority of the views that have been historically entertained by philosophers on ethical questions. I do not mean that there have not been theories which fall outside any of the three groups described; such theories of course have existed, but they have been either unimportant or unphilosophical. By unphilosophical I mean that they have been held by persons who were not accredited philosophers. The Ethics of Swedenborg, and even of Schopenhauer, are not philosophical in the strict sense of the word. They are not tricked out in philosophical garb, they are not defended by dialectical methods, nor are they maintained on logical grounds; more particularly their exact import and significance is not brought out by that discussion and criticism of rival ethical theories which is usual in Philosophy. Jesus Christ also propounded a highly elaborate code of Ethics, but this code has been considered too practical to come within the scope of philosophy, although no community has yet attempted to practise it.

The fact that ethical systems like those of Christ or Schopenhauer do not appear in the usual trappings of philosophical dress, and are not presented by the usual methods of philosophical discourse, does not mean that they are not philosophically important, although it may explain why they have been commonly neglected by philosophers. On the contrary the importance of what I may call these unofficial systems of Ethics is very great, and will be touched

SUMMARY OF ETHICAL THEORIES

upon in later chapters. They frequently draw their inspiration from observation of life, instead of from the manipulation of theory, and gain thereby in freshness and insight what they lose in logical presentation. It is in part to the refusal of philosophical Ethics to take cognizance of such systems, that its barren and abstract nature (of which mention was made in the introduction) may be attributed.

There is a sense, however, in which it may be asserted that systems such as that sketched in the "Sermon on the Mount" are not strictly philosophical, and we may therefore assert that so far as the important philosophical theories which have been propounded with regard to Ethics are concerned, they do in point of fact approximate in type to one of the three main groups of theories described in the first three chapters.

These groups of theories are, with regard to most of the assertions they make, radically different from one another, and philosophers who have held theories belonging to any one of the groups have usually indulged in keen controversy with the supporters of the theories of other groups. The battles waged by J. S. Mill against the critics of Utilitarianism were Homeric.

We have seen that these three groups of theories differ both in the criterion of morality they assert, and in the meaning they apply to the terms good and bad. The Utilitarians believed happiness to be the meaning of good, and the criterion of the morality of actions to depend upon their consequences. The older Intuitionists as a general rule believed virtue to be the meaning of good, and the criterion of the morality of actions to depend upon the approval of the moral sense. Plato and his followers believed the meaning of good to be indefinable, and the criterion of morality to depend upon the presence or the absence of the Form of Good in actions.

The question may be asked whether it is possible to effect any kind of reconciliation between these views apparently so widely divergent.

I think that such a reconciliation is possible, at any rate with regard to the form in which these different theories have been maintained, if not with regard to the spirit which underlies them. A hint that they are not in all respects so irreconcilable as they seem, has already been afforded by an instance of combination presented in a previous chapter. It will be remembered that although we saw reason to adopt the Utilitarian view in so far as it asserted that the rightness and wrongness of actions depended upon their consequences, it was found desirable to resort to some kind of intuition in estimating the value of different kinds of consequences, and there has been in recent times a marked tendency to adopt an Intuitionism of ends or values, in conjunction with a Utilitarian view of the nature of the criterion of rightness and wrongness.

I believe, however, that a more complete combination of these theories can be achieved than the reconciliation which is involved in this selection and combination of one only of the leading propositions of each.

We have seen that the group of theories which were considered under the term "moral sense theories" insisted upon the unique and inalienable character of our judgments of right and wrong. They took the view that the moral sense was a unique instrument directly inherited from God, of which the main function was to deliver ultimate judgments with regard to certain classes of actions and motives. Every human being, it is asserted, possesses this sense in some degree or other, and although it may vary in different periods of the world's history and in different individuals in the same periods, and although it partakes sufficiently of the nature of instinct to be occasionally liable to error, its dictates are not only the most trustworthy guide to what is right and wrong, but they constitute the sole means we possess of distinguishing them. The theory proceeds to draw the inference from the strength and directness of this feeling or intuition, that certain actions must be right and others must be wrong, or we should not all feel so strongly that they are.

Now with regard to the existence of this moral sense there can be no doubt: we have only to look into our own experience for evidence that we do possess it.

The criticism which may be directed against this view does not take the form of denying the existence of the moral sense, but it asserts:

1. That where the moral sense is so largely composed of feeling, and is so obviously subservient to and conditioned by the code of ethics prevalent in a particular community

at a particular time, when in short it is so often purely conventional, it is difficult to regard it as a trustworthy guide to what is really right and really wrong ; and

2. That it is difficult to distinguish any principle of progress in the successive deliverances of the moral senses of successive human communities. The actions of which the moral sense approves and disapproves appear to be chosen in a purely arbitrary manner ; their selection reveals no principle of discrimination between good and bad.

It was also urged that the moral sense of communities has frequently sanctioned the most outrageous actions, which were in the highest degree inimical to human happiness.

Assuming the substance of this criticism to be valid we may assert the following propositions as the outcome of the theories of the moral sense school.

1. Every man has an instinct to call certain things moral. In so far as he does not possess this instinct he is not wholly a man.

2. The nature of the things he will call moral depends almost entirely upon the society in which he happens to live.

Thus if he lives in Turkey he will call the possession of six wives moral : if in England the possession of one only. A Spanish Inquisitor in the sixteenth century would call it moral to roast persons whose views about transubstantiation differed from his own, but in the twentieth century even Father Bernard Vaughan would call such actions immoral.

Similarly the moral promptings of what is called duty vary enormously within the limits of twenty years, encouraging the individual to kill Boers in 1900 if he happens to have been born in England, and Frenchmen in 1918 if he happens to have been born in Germany,—while refusing in peace time to sanction the killing of any one unless he happens previously to have killed some one else.

Turning to the Utilitarian theory, we saw reason to believe that it was correct in asserting that the rightness and wrongness of actions depended upon consequences, but incorrect in asserting that the only consequence of value was happiness. It was incorrect because there are other elements of value besides happiness, the precise proportion in which such elements will be associated in a good life being determined by a further judgment of value.

A right action therefore is that which has consequences of

value in the sense described in Chapter II, while a moral action is that which secures the approval of the moral sense.

Now it is clear that all the actions which have secured the approval of the moral sense have not always had consequences of value, although most of them do have such consequences. It is difficult to describe the burning of heretics or the imprisonment of persons of unpopular political views as actions which have consequences of value. On the other hand, truth-telling, honesty, kindness and tolerance do on the whole have better consequences than lying, dishonesty, cruelty and intolerance. They also obtain the almost universal approval from the moral sense.

Moral actions therefore, in the Intuitionist sense, are not always right actions in the Utilitarian sense: they are, however, usually identical with them.

Now it is reasonable to suppose that if moral progress means anything, it will involve a gradual identification between these two criteria, an increasing identity that is to say between moral actions and right actions. In early stages of society, when the use of force in settling disputes and the right of the stronger prevailed in relations between individuals as well as in relations between nations, actions which were morally approved rarely had the best consequences for mankind as a whole. To-day we may say that, leaving aside exceptional moral judgments such as those which are made in war time, they usually do have such consequences. In an ideal society they would invariably do so.

A society with a high moral standard therefore is one which tends to give the name of moral to those actions which have the best consequences, that is those consequences which contain most elements of value for society as a whole.

We thus get a criterion of morality and a conception of progress in the moral standard, which embodies what is of value both in the Utilitarian and the Intuitionist theories.

It may be asked whether the Platonic theory of the Form of Good has any place in this reconciliation: it seems somehow to stand aloof, perilously near to the preserves of mysticism, alien alike to the hard-headed logic of the theories of Jeremy Bentham and Henry Sidgwick, and to the sentimentalities of some of the moral sense views. It is true that the majority of those who have been attracted by the theory have been of a mystical turn of mind, and have found their satisfaction rather in the aloof majesty and singleness of the Form of Good as an object of contemplation, than in the explanation it affords of the logical problem of the objectivity of morality.

The mystical twist which has been given to the theory is, however, rather the outcome of the proclivities of that school of Plato's followers, known as the Neo-Platonists, than of any intention on the part of Plato. To Plotinus and Porphyry the Form of Good was an object for the contemplation of the mystic, possessing attributes which are more usually associated with the Deity: to Plato it was the ground and explanation of the purely approximate nature of our moral judgments and of the incomplete morality which is all that can be predicated of any physical act. A good action is regarded by Plato as not entirely good but as trying to realize more completely the goodness of the Form which is manifest in it.

Let us endeavour to fit this conception of Plato's, viewed strictly as a logical theory, into the framework of the ethical criterion of which the outlines were sketched above.

In order to do this with any success it is necessary to bear in mind the second and more elaborate conception of the nature and being of the Form of Good which is found in the Republic.

The Form of Good was there conceived of as the source and cause of the existence both of the real world of Forms, and of the half-real world of objects and actions. Progress would therefore mean a more complete approximation on the part of the material world to the Form of Good which is indeed the source of its existence, but whose manifestations are overlaid by matter and distorted by unreality. The Form of Good was also the cause of our knowledge both of the world of Forms, and of the physical world. Growth in our knowledge would therefore be a process of increasing realization of the fundamental truth stripped of irrelevant accretions, that the principle and nature of the Universe is good, and an increasing power of recognition of the Form of Good when it is manifested.

The theory then amounts to a statement of the conviction that the underlying purpose of the Universe is, in spite of all appearance to the contrary, good. It follows from this that morality is not purely arbitrary, nor is our moral sense a purely irresponsible guide, leading us without rhyme and reason to approve of certain actions and to disapprove of others. If the Universe is not a complete hoax, the moral sense must necessarily lead us to approve of those actions which further its real purpose and reflect its real nature: it will lead us to approve therefore of those actions which participate most in the Form of Good.

Now there is no meaning in the conception of good unless, as regards its manifestation in the physical world, it has some bearing upon human welfare. Good is not for Plato a barren and arbitrary concept; actions which are good, in the sense that they participate in the Form, promote human welfare and happiness. It is expressly stated as a matter of fact by Plato that the actions of the just or good man will promote the happiness of his neighbour, and the ideal state which Plato creates in the Republic, whose laws are moulded on the pattern of the Forms of Good and Justice, will produce happy citizens.

We may assume therefore that actions in which the Form of Good is manifest will necessarily tend to be the same as those actions which are called right actions according to the Utilitarian standard, that is actions which have consequences of value; and we may assert this proposition, despite the proviso which it is necessary to make that Plato's idea of value was not in agreement with the theory of a combination in proper proportions of different elements of value described in Chapter II. Plato, who was always anxious to introduce unity into his conceptions, constantly endeavoured to derive all kinds of apparently different values from one supremely valuable thing. This source of supreme value was usually, as we have seen, the Form of Good: sometimes, however, Plato asserts that it is virtue, in other cases he affirms that it is knowledge, while sometimes he speaks of the contemplation of beauty as if it were the only good. Whatever meaning, however, we may give to the word value, it may, I think, be safely assumed that Plato would regard an action which participated in the Form of Good as being one which would have consequences of value. A good action in Plato's sense is therefore identical in this respect with a right action in the Utilitarian sense.

SUMMARY OF ETHICAL THEORIES

It may be, but is not necessarily, identical with a moral action in the Intuitionist sense.

People possess different capacities for recognizing the Form of the Good when it is manifest. We have seen that the deliverances of the moral sense are largely conventional, being for most people conditioned by a slavish acceptance of the code of the community into which they happen to have been born. Thus during the history of mankind every variety of moral judgment has been passed upon the same kind of action.

Now it is clear that the same action cannot both partake and not partake of the Form of Good. No two contrary moral judgments about the same action can therefore be equally correct: one will be more correct than another; the form of the correct judgment being that judgment which approves as moral an action in which the Form of Good is manifest.

Now just as moral progress has been described as an increasing tendency on the part of the moral sense of a community to approve of those actions which are also right actions in the sense that they have consequences of value, so may it with equal truth be described as an increasing tendency to approve of those actions in which the Form of Good is manifest. If a moral action is one which receives the approval of the moral sense, a good action is one in which the Form of Good is manifest. Moral actions are not always good actions, because moral judgments are liable to err, in wrongly detecting the presence of the Form when it is absent. Similarly good actions are not always called moral, because the presence of the Form of Good is not always recognized.

If progress in the moral standard means increasing capacity on the part of society to recognize the presence of the Form of Good, an ideal society will be one in which the presence of the Form is increasingly, and ultimately invariably, recognized. The result will be that actions which obtain the approval of society will be at once those which partake of the Form of Good, and those which have the best consequences.

We have thus established a moral standard and arrived at a meaning for morality which combines the elements of value in each of the three groups of theories we have been considering.

We have reconciled the divergent criteria, which are expressed in the different terms right actions, moral actions, and good actions, and by the introduction of the Form of Good have liberated our moral judgments from the charge of subjectivity.

§ 2. Unreality of Methods Pursued

To many it might seem that such an achievement is of value. It is the main purpose of this book to show that whatever merits or demerits such an exposition and reconciliation of divergent theories may have for the purposes of philosophy, it is of practically no value for the purposes of life.

This may sound like undue modesty on the part of the author. It is perhaps needless to urge that it is not : for the scepticism which is entertained with regard to the value of the above reconciliation applies equally to the conclusions of the various theories which it reconciles, and arises from the particular view with regard to the nature of the result arrived at, and the methods by which it has been reached, which it is the purpose of this book to develop.

The preliminary survey of leading ethical theories upon which we have been engaged has been undertaken mainly in order to throw into relief the scepticism with regard both to the value and significance of their conclusions which the rest of this book will be largely concerned to elaborate : and the composite conclusion with which the survey has ended has been drawn with the same object.

Before proceeding to a more detailed statement of the grounds for this scepticism, I wish to prepare the way by some preliminary remarks about the nature of the reasoning and theorizing upon which I have been engaged. Although these remarks will have reference primarily to the composite conclusion with regard to the meaning of moral progress which I have just reached, they may be taken as applying to each of the ethical theories which have played their part in the formation of that conclusion.

What I have been engaged upon in this chapter is a kind of mental game : the game of making inconsistent theories consistent : to use a more accurate analogy, I have been playing with a kind of mental jigsaw puzzle, in which the component pieces were theories, and of which the object was to fit the pieces into a rounded and complete whole. Where one of the pieces has had a jagged edge which made it unsuitable for the general design, the recalcitrant part has been ruthlessly lopped off, and only that part of the theoretical piece allowed to remain which could be harmoniously fitted into the general scheme.

Now much of philosophy in general, and of ethical philosophy in particular, has been an essay on similar lines in the game of manipulating theories. The object has been to create a logical structure which would be watertight in every compartment, and of which no one part would be inconsistent with any other.

The process is an interesting one, and if successful arrives at a result which is gratifying to the mind. In particular it satisfies the desire for logical unity which is always operative, and which doubtless plays no small part in unconsciously directing the process, with a view to a predestined arrival at the goal to which it points the way.

The important thing to notice, however, is that the process is one in which we drift right away from life, and which leads to conclusions which have no bearing upon life.

The conclusion at which we arrived above is a statement about the nature of certain mental processes : it is not a statement about life. It would only be necessarily true of life, if life were like mathematics. This point is important and needs elaboration.

Many philosophers, particularly those philosophers who belong to what is known as the Rationalist school, have believed that the nature of the Universe was like the nature of mathematics, in the sense that truths about the Universe could be arrived at in the same way as truths about mathematics. Now truths about mathematics can be arrived at by the exercise of the reasoning faculty. If a mathematician were to shut himself up in his study, and to reason about the postulates and axioms of Euclid, he could, provided that his reason was good enough, deduce the whole of the propositions of geometry from those postulates and axioms.

Similarly by reasoning about the properties of integers, he could, again provided that he was sufficiently clever, construct for himself the whole of arithmetic, and it would not be necessary for him to hold intercourse with the world or to correct his results by observation at any stage in the process.

Now if the world is like mathematics, it is clear that truths about the world can be arrived at in the same way, and many philosophers have accordingly believed that the exercise of reason alone, independently of observation, is the proper method for reaching ethical and metaphysical truth.

The world, however, is not like a mathematical problem, and it is accordingly not surprising to find that many ethical theories, however much they may redound to the credit of the reasoning powers of those who evolved them, have no relation to life in the world. Life eludes this mathematical treatment. The properties of the Universe, unlike those of the multiplication table, exhibit a reluctance which, in many cases amounts to a definite refusal, to group themselves under a few comprehensive formulæ which remain universally and unchangeably true. Life is not a static entity whose constancy will ensure that truths discovered about it to-day will necessarily be true next week. Life is changing and dynamic, and any goal which we may set before ourselves is as much subject to change and development as our efforts to reach it.

Rules of conduct and statements of ethical value are themselves conditioned by the changing nature of the material which rules of conduct seek to regulate, and statements of value to estimate. In practical Ethics there is no ultimate criterion of morality just as there is no ultimate good, because human nature perpetually changes, both as regards its conception of right and wrong, and as regards its conception of value.

All that can be said of moral values and moral criteria is that they change. It cannot be said that they progress, for that would involve a conception of a single static goal or good with reference to which their progress could be measured: nor has any age or individual any right to claim finality for the particular good or standard which happens to appeal at the time.

For practical Ethics there are no ultimates.

For theoretical Ethics there may be: such, for example, is the Utilitarian criterion that any action which has the best consequences on the whole is always and universally right. But theoretical Ethics has no direct relation to the problems

SUMMARY OF ETHICAL THEORIES

of life : it is a record of the attitude of the minds of philosophers to those problems.

It is furthermore important to note that by the standard of logical consistency invoked by rationalist philosophical theories (among which many ethical theories may be numbered), it is possible for several contradictory theories to be each of them equally true, because each of them is equally consistent.

If, for example, geometricians were to assume for the starting point of their investigations a number of postulates and axioms which were different from those of Euclid, it would be possible to construct from them an entirely different but equally logical system of geometry. Similarly by altering the accepted scale of notation it is possible to evolve a new arithmetic. Mind has in fact only to start from a number of sufficiently plausible hypotheses to deduce from them a perfectly logical structure on principles which themselves form part of the deduction.

The history of philosophy presents a number of examples of perfectly logical philosophical systems, constructed by philosophers on the assumption that the nature of the Universe, like the nature of mathematics, must necessarily conform to the laws of their own reasoning.

The philosopher Hobbes, for example, on the basis of the hypothesis that every one is naturally selfish, and that every one values security above everything else in the world, constructed an elaborate scheme of political autocracy. Its logical completeness led him to believe that it must necessarily be admirably adapted to the needs of human nature. But in constructing his system he overlooked the fact that in certain circumstances people prefer the dangers of rebellion even to the security of obedience, and the whole structure as a workable political theory is vitiated by Hobbes' neglect of the psychological phenomenon presented by the citizen who voluntarily undergoes the perils of the soldier, in what he believes to be a righteous cause.

Similarly Hegel, reasoning with perfect logic from certain premises with regard to what he assumed to be the nature of the State, produced an elaborate theory of what the State ought to be, and disposed of those critics who pointed out that actually existing States entirely failed to conform to his conception, by bluntly asserting that in so far as existing

States failed to represent the Hegelian picture of what the State ought to be, they were just simply not States. The audacity of this method of punishing life, for refusing to fit into one's preconceived theory of what life ought to be, by bluntly convicting it of not being life, has imposed so completely upon the world that philosophers are still to be found insisting that it is approximation to Hegel's conception, and not the fact of being actually in existence, that confers reality upon States.

But the whole Hegelian conception is vitiated by his neglect of the fact that the State was made for man, instead of man being made for the State, with the result that if a particular state fails to meet the individual's demand for as much freedom as is compatible with order, and insists on complying with Hegel's requirement of as much discipline as the demand for unity and the interest of the rulers requires, it is broken up by the revolt of its disgusted citizens, instead of attaining to a greater degree of reality through its approximation to the Hegelian ideal.

The creation of literary Utopias falls within the same category. A Utopia is the expression of its creator's mind : it is not necessarily a reflection of life, nor does it necessarily embody the desires of men. The authors of Utopias frequently labour under the delusion that the workings of their minds bear a necessary relation to the facts of human aspiration, and are filled with surprise that the mass of men view their ideal societies with repulsion, simply because they do not happen to want to lead the kind of lives that the Utopiast thinks they ought to live.

Theories of this character have no relations, except to the mind from which they emanate. They do not hitch on to the needs of the real world, and the fact that they are entertained does not mean anything more than that a particular mind entertains them. The whole process is like drawing up the rules of a new game of cards which nobody has played, and then expecting people to wish to play it because you have drawn up the rules.

Elaborate theories that evolve absolutes at the expense of the facts are not confined to political philosophy. In metaphysics there have been several theories of this type.

They may roughly be classed under the name of *a priori* theories, that is theories which are based on *a*

SUMMARY OF ETHICAL THEORIES

priori knowledge. By the term *a priori* knowledge is meant that kind of knowledge which is independent of sense experience, and is not derived from it. As applied to these theories, *a priori* means, among other things, that the theories depend on a few general principles of an ultimate character, which are recognized by the mind to be true, but which are not deduced or inferred from any other principles or any other kind of knowledge.

These general principles are intuitively perceived by the mind to be true independently of any evidence: their ultimate nature in fact makes it impossible that any evidence could be adduced in their support, just as propositions such as "health is good," "happiness is better than misery," and other propositions of ultimate value are recognized by the Intuitionists as ultimate truths upon which all Ethics are based. From these general principles philosophers have proceeded to deduce what the nature of the Universe must be, by means of logical laws which are themselves numbered among the principles which are intuitively apprehended by the mind to be true. The process is one which takes place entirely within the philosopher's study, and deductions as to what the nature of the Universe must be are never corrected by a reference to what the nature of the Universe, as it presents itself to the senses, obviously is. In so far as the nature of the Universe, as it is known to the senses, conflicts with *a priori* deductions as to what the nature of the Universe must be, what we know by means of the senses is penalized for its recalcitrance by being convicted of unreality, and labelled as an "appearance," by which is meant a delusive appearance.

Many mathematical systems purporting to state what the nature of the Universe must be have been constituted on these lines,

Descartes, starting from his famous first principle of "*Cogito, ergo sum,*" "I think therefore I exist," deduced by means of the laws of logic the whole structure and nature of the Universe.

Leibnitz constructed a mathematical universe on the basis of a number of homogeneous units, established by logical processes, called monads.

The most striking example of this tendency is, however, afforded by Hegel's theory of the Absolute, which has been developed in England by the philosophers, Mr. Bradley and Mr. Bosanquet.

According to Hegel there is only one thing in the Universe which is absolutely real: this thing is the Absolute. All existing things which appear to be real are only partially so: upon investigation by Hegel's logical method they show themselves to be riddled with contradictions. Not only are things not real in their own right, but they are not really distinct and different from one another as they appear to be. Logical examination shows all apparent differences to be as partial and unreal as the things they differentiate. There is no distinction between mind and its objects, just as there is no distinction between any two physical objects. Mind itself, in the sense of the individual's mind, being partial is not truly real, and because of its imperfect reality it necessarily entertains a view of the Universe which is also partial and incomplete. This incompleteness of view is the cause of the apparent diversity which the universe presents to us, and the reason why we attribute reality to finite individual things. The view which a divine intelligence would have of the Universe would show all these apparent differences to be delusive, and would reveal the Universe as perfect unity and oneness. This perfect unity and oneness is the Absolute; but as, short of the Absolute, there is no being possessed of a sufficient comprehension of view to realize the oneness and perfection which is the Absolute, the Absolute is not only the sum total of reality known, but the sum total of the mind or minds which know it. The Absolute reconciles therefore the differences between knowing mind and known matter, by asserting them to be ultimately one, a oneness in which perfect reality and perfect knowledge of that reality are united. The ultimate reality is therefore mental in structure, and matter is a delusion.

It may be asked what this apparent digression upon rationalist metaphysical systems in general, and Hegel's system of the Absolute in particular, has to do with the ethical conclusions arrived at in this chapter, and the stigma of unreality which, in an apparently dogmatic manner, I have placed upon them.

The connection is not far to seek.

Concurrently with the rationalist movement in metaphysics there has grown up what is known as the empirical

SUMMARY OF ETHICAL THEORIES

school. This school has roundly asserted that all knowledge is derived from some sense experience, has denied the existence of intuitively apprehended general principles, or has at least denied their validity as guides to the nature of the Universe, and has in some cases impugned the validity even of the so-called laws of logic by means of which the rationalists have constructed their systems on the basis of their general principles. In reply to the rationalist proofs of what the nature of the Universe must be, they have asserted that you must go and see what the nature of the Universe is, and their observation has led them to widely different conclusions.

Locke, with his attack on the "innate ideas" of Descartes, was the first of the important empiricists. Berkeley and Hume followed in his footsteps, and the main tradition of English philosophy has been empirical, as opposed to the rationalist tradition of the Germans. To-day under the influence of William James the chief upholders of the empiricist school come from America.

This empiricist movement, which is largely in the nature of a reaction, has had a profound effect upon metaphysics.

It scarcely seems to have touched philosophical Ethics.

Yet in no sphere of philosophy has *a priori* rationalization been so prevalent. All the ethical theories which we have been considering base themselves on *a priori* principles which are regarded as intuitively known, and from these principles are constructed by logical steps the theories described in the first three chapters. These general principles are as a rule principles of ethical value, such as that knowledge is more desirable than ignorance, happiness than misery, goodwill than hatred. The intrusion of experience is only admitted by these theories, because our knowledge of these principles can only be elicited by experience. Ethical values are not realized until we have had some experiences of the world; but when experience has once turned our mind towards the truth, as Plato would put it, our knowledge of these values is seen to be independent of experience, and incapable either of proof or disproof by experience.

From this point onward no appeal is made to experience in ethical theorizing, which proceeds by a manipulation of theories and arguments, which is at no stage corrected by reference to life, and of which our method of arriving at the logical amalgam of theories which formed our conclusion earlier in the chapter, affords a good example.

The conclusion which we reached is like the conclusion of Hobbes about the State, or Hegel about the Absolute. Although it may possess a kind of logical truth, it fails to apply itself to the problem of actual life.

In order to arrive at a conception of Ethics which will bear a direct relation to life, we must start as the empiricists did in metaphysics with observation instead of with general principles. Ethics will become therefore more psychological than it has been in the past, and will devote itself to observing what people do in fact desire.

Its conclusions will be provisional instead of ultimate, and fluid instead of static. We shall arrive at no one good which is good for all men in all ages, and no one criterion of right and wrong which is valid for all men in all ages.

On the contrary we shall draw up a sort of catalogue of elements of value which will be true, in so far as it is true, only of the particular age in which we live, and we shall experience no disappointment if the items in our catalogue fail to group themselves under a few comprehensive formulæ.

An indication of the lines upon which such an inquiry into empirical or common-sense Ethics should proceed, will be given in the following chapters.

PART II

EMPIRICAL OR COMMON-SENSE ETHICS

CHAPTER V

THE PSYCHOLOGY OF IMPULSE

§ 1. Relation of Ethics to Psychology and Politics

THE last chapter concluded by setting before the student of what I have called empirical Ethics the task of drawing up a catalogue of elements of value, the standard of value being nothing more nor less than what is in fact desired.

It is not possible within the limits of this book to attempt to compile such a catalogue, nor is the task one which could be attempted without an adequate psychological equipment. Our desires are elusive things; they are rarely simple, and they are frequently cheats. A desire for something which is commonly regarded as disreputable, disguises itself in a properly conducted mind, and masquerades as a desire for something else, while many if not most of our desires are unconscious and are only revealed by psycho-analysis or by some analogous process.

In formulating our list of ethical values with reference to the facts of desire, it would be necessary to rule out fictitious desires, and to bring to the surface those desires which are unconscious, and a thorough understanding of the works of such writers as Freud and Jung would be an indispensable preliminary to the inquiry.

The most that I can hope to do in this and the following chapters will be to give an indication of the method to be pursued in such an inquiry, by directing attention to the ethical significance of one or two aspects of human psychology which appear to have been somewhat overlooked by philosophers. The conclusions at which I hope to arrive should not be regarded as providing a complete contents list of the catalogue of ethical values, but they will at least furnish the catalogue with one or two very important entries.

It is clear in the first place that an ethical inquiry which is conducted on empirical lines will be more closely related to other sciences than traditional philosophical Ethics has been in the past. In particular it will poach extensively on the preserves both of psychology and of politics. As regards psychology it will be remembered that we drew attention in the last chapter to the methods of the empirical metaphysicians Locke and Hume. In contradistinction to the rationalistic speculations of their predecessors, which asserted what the nature of the Universe must, according to the laws of reasoning, necessarily be, these philosophers insisted that the philosopher must go and see what the nature of the Universe really was. Similarly if we hold that any attempt to lay down by *a priori* reasoning what the nature of the good must be, or to deduce the nature of the criterion which distinguishes right from wrong from certain data which are regarded as unchangeable, is bound to lead to conclusions which are unrelated to life, we have no alternative but to go to life itself, and observe what people's experience pronounces to be good, and what they appear to mean by morality.

Our question becomes in the first place, " What do men in fact desire ? " and in the second, " Which of their desires make for those things which are as a matter of fact universally regarded as good, as for instance happiness and freedom ? " These are questions of psychology, and it is from the observations of psychologists that we must borrow material for the inquiry. The task is complicated by the complexity of the phenomena of human desire. Man is a complex machine, and to discover his real views on ethical value we must take him to pieces and see what he is made of.

Our relation to politics is equally close.

If we hold that there is no one good which can be discovered by reasoning about the nature of the good, and no one criterion of right and wrong which remains inalienably the same, it follows that our ideas of good and our ideas of morality will be subject to constant change. Furthermore there will be many goods instead of one, and many different conceptions of the relation between right and wrong, each of which may be equally correct at the time.

Now people are invariably influenced in their notions both of good and of morality by the community in which they live. Apart from the influence of public opinion the community may in certain cases consciously direct and mould the individual's ideas of good and right, and may devise systems and institutions which to a greater or less degree make it possible for him to realize his conception of good, and to live up to his conception of right. A community, for instance, which allows a man to starve who happens to hold the view that stealing is wrong and respect for property right, does not make it easy for him to live up to his moral principles when he sees an unwatched leg of mutton hanging outside a butcher's shop.

It is not sufficient then for us to ask what it is that men do desire: we must go on to inquire how their desires may be realized and their ideals achieved? This is largely a question of politics. Some political systems make the possibility of a good life much easier to realize than others: some make a good life as it is usually conceived almost impracticable.

In England to-day the political system is more favourable to the realizations of a life of ethical value than the despotism exercised in Russia under the Tsar. But it is pertinent to inquire whether any other social system could in theory be devised which would be more likely to achieve the desired result than the present one. Reverting to Schopenhauer's definition of human society, as a collection of hedgehogs driven together for the sake of warmth, we may regard it as the business of politics to blunt the bristles, and so by means of greater proximity to increase the warmth.

I propose to consider in this chapter the relation of Ethics to Psychology, and in the next the relation of Ethics to Politics.

§ 2. Is Ethics Simply a Catalogue of Desires?

It may be asked at the outset whether the reduction of Ethics to a mere catalogue of what is actually desired leaves any room for Ethics at all.

It may be argued that if all you mean by the good is what is desired, if in fact good and desired are equivalent and interchangeable terms, the only criterion of good is intensity of desire, while right and wrong cease to have any meaning. You cannot say that some desires are good because they achieve good ends, while others are bad because they achieve bad ends : all desires are equally desires ; all desires are therefore, with the exception of degrees of intensity, equally desirable, which means that all desires are equally good.

Intensity of desire is therefore the only measure of value.

It follows from this line of argument that the statement made above, that it is necessary to find out which of our desires make for happiness, freedom, and other things which are universally approved, involves a superfluous inquiry. The inquiry is superfluous, says the critic, because inasmuch as the objects of all desire, in virtue of the fact that they are objects of desire, are upon the premises you have been assuming, all equally good, there is nothing to be gained by separating off certain of those objects such as happiness and freedom, and saying that the desires which pursue them are ethically good and important, in some sense in which other desires are not good and important.

If on the other hand you assert (the argument continues) that happiness and freedom are in some unique and distinctive way good and valuable, and the desires which pursue them ought therefore to be encouraged while contrary desires ought to be suppressed, you are guilty of the same kind of *a priori* rationalizing for which you have been indicting other philosophers. You are segregating two elements which are undoubtedly valuable as though they possessed ultimate objective and unchanging value, quite irrespective of the different sentiments which people in different ages have entertained towards them, and the different values which different people in the same age may ascribe to them, the prisoner regarding freedom as the only good and counting happiness merely as an incidental appanage of it, while a man in the throes of sciatica insists that cessation of pain is the only good, remaining indifferent to happiness or freedom, both of which he regards as superfluous irrelevancies.

This is an important objection, and I must hasten to clear

myself of the charge of *a priori* rationalizations about value.

By instancing happiness and freedom as objects of desires which should be encouraged, I do not mean to suggest that they alone of all the things which are desired are really desirable in the sense that they alone *ought* to be desired; nor do I mean that there is anything fundamentally unique or important about happiness and freedom in the sense that they can be shown by a process of logical deduction to be the only true objects of desire, while other desires resolve themselves on analysis into desires for happiness and freedom.

I do not mean in fact to argue as the Utilitarians have argued that because a visit to a concert to hear Beethoven's Fifth Symphony gives me pleasure, the motive which took me to the concert was therefore the desire for pleasure, and not the desire to hear music, and that all apparent desires for other things are in a similar way really desires for the pleasure which the attainment of those other things will bestow. I think on the contrary that there are a number of things which are desired for their own sake, and that any attempt to analyze these desires into desires for other and more ultimate things, for the sake of which the first things are desired, though it is logically irrefutable, is a falsification of what actually happens in the psychology of the person entertaining the desire.

I cited happiness and freedom not as being the only two real objects of desire, but simply as two instances of things which are in fact desired for their own sake, and I base this statement not on a process of logical reasoning showing that all other kinds of desires can be resolved into desires for happiness and freedom, but on observation.

The statement is an empirical generalization, which appears to be true on the whole of most men at the present time. It is not put forward as an *a priori* principle which is necessarily true for all men and holds good for all time.

The statement is in fact analogous to the kind of assertion made by empirical metaphysicians when rebutting the logical reasoning of those who seek to prove that there can be no such thing as knowledge. "The fact that you can show by argument," they retort, "that there is no such thing as knowledge is not of any importance. You can by means of argument in these matters arrive at any conclusion to which your iconoclastic temperament naturally predisposes you. Although it may be impossible for us to prove that there is such a thing as knowledge, since to do so would involve the assumption of the validity of that very knowledge which we should be trying to establish, nevertheless we have not the slightest doubt about the facts that *we do know*, and also that *we know that we know*."

Similarly I am assuming not only that people do as a rule desire happiness and freedom, but also that they know roughly what they mean by these terms. The latter assumption is convenient not only because it enables me to assume that everybody means roughly the same thing by the terms happiness and freedom, but also because it avoids the necessity of having to evolve complex definitions with which everybody would be anxious to quarrel.

The assumption that people desire, among other things, happiness and freedom involves on my premises the further assumption that that conduct is ethically good which tends to promote them, and that conduct ethically bad which tends to impede them. We have therefore, in taking to pieces the human machine, to pick out those psychological elements which make for happiness and freedom, as elements to be encouraged, and to indicate those which make against them as elements which ought to be discouraged.

In this way it is hoped to indicate the lines upon which empirical Ethics should proceed : it will start, that is, on the basis of what is generally desired, and will then proceed to ascribe ethical value to those desires and those lines of conduct which bring these generally approved ends nearer, and to condemn on ethical grounds those which oppose their realization. I must, however, be excused for again pointing out that as this book does not purport to give an exhaustive treatment of empirical or common-sense Ethics, but only to indicate a method to be pursued, I have only selected instances of valuable ends in citing happiness and freedom, and I am only going to cite one very important instance of the kind of life and conduct which seems to me likely to promote them. I am not covering the whole field of value, but selecting certain ends of value only, and I am not treating of all the kinds of conduct and desire likely to promote these selected ends, but am proposing to emphasize one element of psychology which appears to me to have been overlooked, although it is of great importance for the attainment of these ends.

§ 3. Distinction between Impulse and Desire

The element of human psychology which I desire to emphasize as having an important bearing on the realization of happiness and freedom, is that element which is summed up in the use of the word " impulse."

I do not propose at this stage to give a definition of impulse, partly because it is not definable in strict terms of logic, and partly because it is more convenient to define a thing when you have finished talking about it, rather than when you begin. Every definition begs the question at issue in the sense that it presupposes the truth of that particular view of the entity in question which you are proposing to adopt ; and although the reasons given in the course of your discussions may not completely justify the particular form of question-begging you adopt in your definition, it nevertheless creates a better impression to beg the question after you have given at length your reasons for doing so, than it does to beg it by defining your terms at the beginning.

The value of impulse is brought out in a significant way by a distinction which Mr. Bertrand Russell draws between impulse and desire.

" All human activity," says Mr. Russell, " springs from two sources, impulse and desire." Speaking of desire he says, " When men find themselves not fully contented, and not able instantly to procure what will cause content, imagination brings before their mind the thought of things which they believe would make them happy. All desire involves an interval of time between the consciousness of a need and the opportunity for satisfying it. The acts inspired by desire may be in themselves painful. . . . Will as a directing force consists mainly in following desires for more or less distant objects, in spite of the painfulness of the acts involved and the solicitations of incompatible but more immediate desires and impulses."

Speaking of impulse as opposed to desire, Mr. Russell continues : " In all the more instinctive parts of our nature we are dominated by impulses to certain kinds of activity, not by desires for certain ends. Children run and shout not because of any good which they expect to realize, but because of a direct impulse to running and shouting. Dogs bay at the moon not because they consider that it is their advantage to do so, but because they feel an impulse to bark. It is not any purpose that prompts such actions as eating, drinking, love-making, quarrelling, boasting."

As preliminary distinctions then we may note the following characteristics of desires and impulses respectively:

1. Desires are for conscious ends. Impulses, even where we are conscious of them, are not towards any specific end. Desires for ends of which we are not conscious may more properly be termed impulses.

2. Desires involve a need, and a lapse of time between feeling the need and its satisfaction. Impulses also involve a need, but in so far as the need is satisfied, it is satisfied so soon as it is felt.

3. Desires usually invoke the aid of the will to subdue contrary desires and impulses which impede their accomplishment. Impulses do not involve the use of will and are not helped by it; they are only related to will in so far as they are repressed by will.

4. The fulfilment of an impulse always brings immediate pleasure. The pursuit of desires frequently involves pain during the period before the end is achieved.

It is not claimed that this distinction between impulse and desire can always be upheld if it is subjected to strict logical analysis; it is a distinction based rather on observation than deduced by reasoning, and is not therefore completely watertight. For practical purposes, however, it will serve well enough, and although certain classes of impulses and desires may shade into one another (and indeed I hope to show later that many so-called desires are in their real nature more closely akin to impulses), the distinction is as a rule clear-cut enough. Thus as a typical example of desire, we may take the case of the boy who desires to pass an examination, and in order that he may get through the necessary work subdues his desire to go to the cinema. As a typical example of impulse, we may take the feeling which prompts some Londoners to get out into the country at all costs on the first fine morning in spring. In these two cases the distinction is obviously clear enough.

While the importance of desire has been generally recognized in Philosophy, the importance of impulse has been much overlooked. The result has had a profound effect on the philosophy both of politics and Ethics, which have been based almost entirely upon the phenomena of desire, and make scarcely any provision for the satisfaction of impulse. It is upon the recognition and encouragement of the life of impulse that I wish to lay emphasis in indicating those elements in the make-up of the human machine, which seem to me to be ethically valuable,—valuable, that is, in the sense that they tend to promote desirable ends such as happiness and freedom.

I think we can distinguish four reasons why philosophers have overlooked the importance of impulse in forming their ethical systems. The first two of these reasons, though they have exercised a sufficiently important influence, are of a comparatively superficial character, and can be treated briefly. The other two are more significant, and as they throw considerable light not only on the nature of impulse and desire, but also on the unconscious motives underlying the traditional systems of *a priori* Ethics which we have been considering in earlier chapters, I shall treat them in some detail.

Man's Belief that Man is Rational

1. Most men have a predilection in favour of believing that they are rational creatures, inspired in the main by desires for rational ends.

Even Aristotle's proof that reason was the servant of desire, in the sense that desire sets the end and reason discovers the necessary steps for its achievement, was at first received with incredulity owing to the implied aspersion upon reason. When it was admitted that some form of desire was the mainspring of all action, it became necessary to save the face of reason by showing that reason as the servant of desire was engaged on a reputable task. The phrase rational desire was therefore coined, to indicate that the ends which desire set reason to achieve were of a creditable character, for which good arguments could be found. It has usually been thought that most human activity, though occasionally misguided, was yet in a position to give a sufficiently rational account of itself and to justify itself, at any rate to its author, on grounds which could pass muster as reasonable without undue self-deception. Irrational action was accordingly supposed to be the special prerogative of animals, or at best of women, whose irrational impulses and capacity for what is called intuition were referred to in terms of condescension, as betokening an inferiority in that capacity for rational conduct which is regarded as specifically male.

The enunciation and general acceptance of the theory of evolution has only intensified this prejudice in favour of the belief that most of our actions are rational.

The discovery of our near relationship, as regards most of our characteristics, to the animal creation, rendered it doubly important to emphasize our power of rational action, as the only feature of real distinction and superiority which was left to us.

There has always existed therefore an instinctive impulse to repress any suggestion that the mainspring of our actions was to be found in the generality of cases rather in instinctive impulse than in rational desire. Samuel Butler records of his father that he never would admit to himself that he did anything because he wished to. The whole tenor of our upbringing and education is to make us despise and distrust instinct and impulse, and to disguise from ourselves the enormous extent to which they prompt our actions.

Thwarted Impulses become Desires

2. Mr. Russell points out that when an impulse is repressed we immediately desire the results which would have attended the indulgence of the impulse. By frustrating what is originally an impulse we transform it into a desire.

Impulses therefore " bring with them a whole train of fictitious desires : they make men feel that they desire the results which will follow from indulging the impulses, and that they are acting for the sake of these results, when in fact their action has no motive outside itself."

A man will walk ten miles across country in the belief that he desires to inspect some antique carving in the church of a remote village. But when he arrives at the church he finds that the carving has little interest for him, and that the real motive of his ten-mile walk was the impulse towards open-air exercise and exploration. He would not perform a similar feat with a similar fictitious object if the way lay through the streets of a London suburb.

Thus we habitually interpret to ourselves actions whose real motive is impulse, as actions prompted by a specific desire, and in this way the importance of impulse is overlooked.

Does Consciousness Exist?

3. A new light has been thrown upon the psychology of impulse and desire by the work of the psycho-analysts, such as Freud and Jung on the one hand, and the Behaviourist school of Psychologists on the other. The work of these two schools of thinkers has profoundly modified our view of consciousness.

The ordinary view of consciousness, held for example by the writers on Ethics whose theories we have been considering, presupposed as the basis of desire a consciously conceived object, which embodied the purpose of the desire. In the desire to pass an examination, for example, it was supposed that there existed, to begin with, a clearly-defined conception of the results of passing the examination, which prompted the desire to pass.

The investigations of psycho-analysts, however, have shown that many if not most of our desires are unconscious, and that there is no necessity for a conception of the result or purpose of the desire to enter into consciousness in order that the desire should exist. The phenomena associated with multiple personality make the results of these investigations even more significant, and it is impossible to explain either these phenomena or the fact of unconscious desire on the basis of the ordinary psychology which regards desire as presupposing a consciously conceived end or purpose.

Among certain modern schools of psychology, the significance of these phenomena has been used as the basis for a complete denial of the existence of consciousness, as a unique and separate item in the human make-up.

The Behaviourist Psychology

It is argued, for instance, by the psychologists known as Behaviourists that since people are shown by the experiments of psycho-analysts to be unconscious of desires and thoughts which are apparently being entertained by them, being able, for example, unconsciously to remember all sorts of occurrences of which they are unaware, it is not a necessary condition of normal behaviour, that the agent should be conscious of his behaviour. It is not therefore necessary that self-consciousness should exist at all. It is true that we invariably think and speak of ourselves as acting for certain definite ends and desiring certain definite objects. But these apparent desires are the result of later reflection which rationalizes a purely instinctive impulse into desire for an end. The end exists only for an outside spectator who, observing the phenomena which result when a person is acting under an impulse or an unconscious desire, and noting that the activity in question frequently results in the attainment of an end or state which is pleasant, describes the whole process as resulting from an original desire for that end or state. But this is a description based on the appearance the process presents to an observer. It is not an accurate psychological account of the process.

It should be noted that for thinkers of this school there is no such thing as Introspection: that is to say, it is held to be impossible for any person, by means of what is called Introspection or by any other means, to acquire a knowledge of himself other than and additional to the knowledge which other persons may obtain from observing him from outside.

It follows therefore that when we refer to the fictitious appearance which a person's motives and actions present to outside observers, fictitious because leading them to interpret actions proceeding from unconscious impulses, as actions prompted by a conscious desire for an end, we must include the agent himself as one of the outside observers. Hence arises on the part of the agent that mistaken identification of impulses with conscious desires, of which we are all guilty when observing our own psychology.

There is reason to suppose that this identification is facilitated by the habit of language which in describing actions insists on speaking of actions of such-and-such a character, as desires for such-and-such objects. Thus we do not say that X acted in such-and-such a way when we observed him running to catch a train this morning: what we do say is that X desired to catch such-and-such a train, and it is inferred from this statement that the motive of his action was a conscious desire to catch the train.

This is not the place for a detailed discussion of the

merits of Behaviourist psychology. It is sufficient to point out here that if it is correct in *all* that it asserts it renders Ethics impossible. That this result follows from Behaviourist premises it is not difficult to show.

As expounded by its most thorough-going supporters, it is a theory which holds that the only data which can legitimately exist for psychology are those which can be obtained from an observation of animal and human behaviour. It follows therefore that there is no reason to assume that there is anything in the human mental make-up beyond what can be observed : for anything additional to what can be observed, such as consciousness, is sheer inference from observation, and unwarranted inference at that.

Now the sum total of the phenomena of human behaviour which can be observed is a series of stimuli producing a series of reactions. We infer that these stimuli pass into consciousness and produce certain effects : one of these effects may be the will to perform the actions which the psychologist observes ; another may be a thought process which results in a number of figures being written on a piece of paper ; but since neither the consciousness, nor the will, nor the thought process can be observed, the Behaviourist simply denies their existence. We may, for instance, have thought ourselves justified in supposing that when we produce a pound note in payment for a pair of stockings priced at 8s. 11$\frac{3}{4}d$., we do a rapid mental calculation before we assert that 11s. 0$\frac{1}{4}d$. is the change due to us. The Behaviourist denying the mental calculation because it cannot be observed, explains the demand for 11s. 0$\frac{1}{4}d$. by attributing it to the fact that we have acquired certain habits of speech, which prompt us to enunciate the words eleven shillings and a farthing, when giving a name to the series of automatic reactions caused by the respective stimuli, of a pound note, a pair of stockings, and the price of 8s. 11$\frac{3}{4}d$.

The result is to abolish will, consciousness, and thought, and to explain the whole of human activity as a series of reactions to the outside world. Thus we arrive at a form of psychological determinism which reduces our personality to a series of desires for which we are not responsible, resulting in a series of actions which are only by courtesy called ours.

There is no place for Ethics in such a psychology. Ethics necessarily involves the admission of the principles of free will, and of human responsibility; it stands upon the twin pedestals of praise and blame; and if we remove those pedestals by eliminating the will which makes people responsible for their actions, and regard human beings merely in the light of mediums for the registering of external stimuli, Ethics falls to the ground.

But although we may refuse to swallow the whole of the Behaviourist psychology, we must admit that that part of it which emphasizes the scope and significance of unconscious desire by restricting the province of the will to the comparatively small sphere left for conscious desire, considerably diminishes the field of our activity over which Ethics may claim to exert a sway.

It will be remembered that one of the main distinctions drawn above between desire and impulse was that desire presupposed a definite end consciously conceived as the motive for action, while impulse sprang up spontaneously and was devoid alike of end and purpose. Impulse is a push from behind, whereas desire is a pull from in front. Now unconscious desires fall within the same category as impulses, in the sense that they do not involve any purpose or prevision of an end, and prompt actions of whose real motive the author is unconscious.

Impulse is in fact only another name for unconscious desire. I do not mean by this that we are always unconscious of our impulses: we are all of us, for instance, conscious of an impulse to sing in our bath; but impulse is the name we frequently give to the promptings of an unconscious desire when we become aware of them, and these promptings, like the unconscious desire which produced them, are not directed to achieving any consciously conceived end.

Importance of Unconscious Desires

Unconscious desires and the impulses which they produce are of the greatest importance for psychology; and the fact that they have been so largely neglected, or interpreted as conscious desires—a neglect which has profoundly affected the views of philosophers about the facts of human motive— makes them equally important for our study of Ethics.

Before, however, we are in a position to establish their sig-

THE PSYCHOLOGY OF IMPULSE 109

nificance and importance, it is necessary to examine a little more closely why they have been so generally overlooked.

Unconscious desires presuppose a state of restlessness or unsatisfied want. This state of restlessness prompts a series of actions which persist until the want is satisfied and the restlessness allayed. This result which brings the series of actions to an end is usually called the purpose of the series of actions. The word purpose is, however, misleading, because it conveys the impression that the result achieved was a definite end, consciously pursued by the author of the actions, and serving as a motive for the actions. But the mere fact that a series of actions persists until a so-called end is achieved, does not mean that the end was ever consciously pursued, and indeed with regard to most of our actions this is not the case. The end is in most cases simply a series of pleasant sensations. These pleasant sensations, by allaying the unpleasant sensations, which produced the feeling of restlessness, which in turn produced the series of acts, bring the series of acts to a close. The notion of purposiveness in the series of acts, a notion which causes the series of pleasant sensations to be described as an end, with all that the word end connotes, is a mental construction, the result of later reflection upon a series of phenomena. The later reflection thinks of the whole series as purposed from the beginning and therefore rational, because the effect of reflection is to rationalize the instinctive: but such an account is not in most cases a correct version of psychological history. It explains, however, why many actions springing from unconscious desires are regarded as actions prompted by desires for specific ends.

There are of course cases in which our desires are conscious, and are consciously directed to a particular end; but although as civilization advances these cases increase in number, they are still in a minority. Actions proceeding from so-called conscious desires may be described as series of actions which are prompted by an unconscious desire in the way already described, with the addition of a true judgment or belief in the agent's mind as to the so-called object of the series of actions. In the case of familiar desires our belief as to the end in question is usually correct: in the case of new desires we frequently have a mistaken belief as to the nature of the end, and it may be noted as a curious but not uncommon complication, that a false judgment or belief as to the purpose or end of a desire frequently produces a real desire for the false end which our judgment attributed to the series of acts prompted by the former desire.

Thus it is notorious that the attraction which takes many unmarried women to church, is the quasi-satisfaction which the practice of religion affords to thwarted sex instinct. Although they entertain what is originally a false belief as to the motive which prompted the series of church-going acts, attributing them to a desire for the consolations of religion, people of this class in course of time frequently experience a real desire for the end which they innocently believed themselves to be pursuing in the first instance, so that the originally false belief as to the motive of the series of acts becomes a true one.

In the case of most of our desires, however, the process by which we attribute to them design or purpose is a misleading one. Putting the matter shortly we may say that we come to attribute consciously pursued ends to unconscious desires and impulses:

(*a*) Because the process of subsequent reflection causes the notion of an originally conceived purpose to be applied to the pleasant sensations which conclude a series of acts springing from a state of restlessness.

(*b*) Because the ends which we falsely believe to be the objects of a series of unconscious desires, frequently become in course of time the real objects of desire.

(*c*) Because when an unconscious desire or impulse is thwarted, a conscious desire does in fact spring up for the results which would have attended the fulfilment of the impulse.

It will be seen from the above considerations why it is that while the part played by conscious desire has been considerably over-rated in psychology, the part played by impulse has been generally overlooked.

The above conclusion with regard to the scope of unconscious desire has an important bearing upon Ethics. If most of our actions are the results of a push from behind and not of a pull from in front, the traditional ethical systems with which we have been dealing in the earlier chapters are for the most part beside the point. They erect criteria by which, as we have seen, the value of actions is estimated either with reference to the motive with which they are performed, or to the end which the agent pursues, or to the consequences which the actions produce. But if most of our actions are the result of impulse or desires which are unconscious, it is clear that they are not performed with any motive, nor do they seek to achieve any end.

The Intuitionist or Moral Sense theories therefore, which insist that motives or ends must be taken into account, establish criteria which are completely irrelevant to the great majority of our actions. Their standard of value will not work, simply because the considerations which it takes into account are not there. To apply the moral sense criterion to the actions which proceed from impulse and unconscious desire, is like getting a six-foot ruler to measure the quantity of bad temper in men with red hair.

The Utilitarian theories fare little better when applied to the psychology of impulse. It is true that they make their criterion of the rightness and wrongness of actions independent of the psychological state of the agent. Whether the agent did or did not intend to produce the consequences which in point of fact followed from his action does not, according to these theories, affect the ethical value of the actions, and questions of aim and motive are therefore irrelevant. But the Utilitarians, as will be remembered, erected a series of moral " oughts " on the basis of their principle that everybody " ought " to promote the greatest happiness of the greatest number; and in working out this principle they introduced another " ought " by asserting that everybody ought to be reckoned as one, and nobody as more than one, and so forth. These " oughts " presuppose the phenomenon of conscious desire on the part of the agent, namely the ever present desire to promote the greatest happiness of the greatest number, and in so far as his actions are not continually prompted by this conscious desire he is accounted morally blameworthy.

But it is absurd to blame a man for what he cannot help, and if most of his desires are unconscious he cannot be expected to be responsible for them: he cannot even be responsible for checking them, because *ex hypothesi* he does not know they are there; and he cannot be held as responsible for the actions which proceed from them. Now it is essential for ethical systems that they should be able to administer praise and blame for observance or non-observance of the criteria which they set up.

As applied therefore to the majority of our actions the criteria of the Intuitionist and Utilitarian systems are meaningless. They involve the presupposition that our actions are rational and are prompted by the desire for ends consciously conceived, and they make ethical merit dependent upon the selection of good ends instead of bad ones, and the unremitting pursuit of the good ends selected.

Like most *a priori* theories they fail to apply to the problems of life, because they are constructed irrespective of the facts of psychology. According to the criteria which these theories have set up, most of our actions are ethically neither good nor bad : they are ethically neutral. Faced therefore with the failure of the old standards to apply to actions proceeding from impulse and unconscious desire, it is clear that we must look in other directions for the ethical standard, if any, which we are to apply to actions of this class.

How Impulse Conditions Beliefs

4. A further set of reasons can, I think, be distinguished for the comparative neglect of the importance of impulses by ethical writers. These reasons are of a different class from those we have just considered. We have been dealing with impulse as a motive to action: we have now to consider its influence in the formation of belief. There is a kind of conspiracy to ignore the part played by impulse in conditioning beliefs. What are the reasons for this state of affairs?

We have seen how in the sphere of conduct men, wishing to believe that their actions were prompted by rational desire, have been reluctant to ascribe them to instinctive impulse. In the sphere of thought, which should more properly be called belief, this reluctance is greatly increased. Even if men can be brought to admit that their actions are frequently not rational, few men are rational enough to admit that the same is true of their beliefs. Yet the part played by impulse in governing our beliefs appears to be as important as its rôle in prompting our actions.

I have dealt elsewhere with this subject, in an essay on the importance of temperament in conditioning thought. It is argued in this essay that with a few exceptions in favour of mathematics and certain propositions about morality, our intellectual beliefs spring from and are conditioned almost wholly by our temperaments. Temperament is fundamental and is responsible both for what we want and what we feel. It is the function of reason to invent justifications and excuses for what we naturally want to do, and arguments for what we naturally want to believe. Thus what we believe depends very largely upon what we feel, and our intellectual beliefs, instead of being, as we fondly imagine, freely formed by reason, upon an impartial investigation of the evidence for and against the belief in question, are unconsciously dictated by our natural impulses, which predispose us to certain beliefs rather than to others.[1]

Now by temperament I mean the sum total of our various impulses, inherited, acquired, instinctive and so forth, and I have tried to show in the discussion referred to that the influence of this factor of temperament may be most clearly discerned in our religious and political beliefs. The experience of giving a course of lectures on this subject has shown the writer that it is difficult to evolve any conclusion which is more repugnant to the human mind.

It has been pointed out above that people are taught to despise and distrust their impulses, and to be sentimentally proud of their reason. They like to think of the latter as free; it is to them a guiding and controlling power; a sort of a charioteer holding the reins that guide the various impulses, able to indulge and to check them at will, and as life proceeds obtaining increasing control over his unruly steeds.

As a result there are few beliefs more repugnant to a proper pride in reason than the belief that our beliefs are moulded and conditioned by our impulses, are in fact little more than rationalizations of them.

Yet in the sphere of Ethics, no less than in politics and religion, this seems to be pre-eminently the case.

Morality as the Impulse to Blame

Most ethical systems arise from the impulse to blame.

[1] See for a fuller discussion of the subject my "Essays in Common-Sense Philosophy," Chapter on Thought and Temperament.

This impulse is a very strong and a very important one. It is sufficiently strong to account for most of our taboos, and for a large part of our morality. Let us see how this result is brought about?

The origin and growth of many of our moral maxims must have followed some such course as the following. If we revert once more to Schopenhauer's definition of human society as a collection of hedgehogs driven together for the sake of warmth, it is obvious that many will find their quarters uncomfortably close. Other people will be continually performing actions which are inconvenient to the individual personally : sometimes they will be irritating to the community as a whole.

The individual feels an impulse to disapprove of such actions, and, if he can obtain the support of his neighbours, will get society to stigmatize the action as wrong. In extreme cases it will become punishable by law. In less extreme cases the disapproval of society expressed in what is called public opinion is usually sufficient to prevent its repetition.

The important point to notice is that the action is regarded as ethically wrong only because somebody in the first instance had an impulse to blame its author for doing something inconvenient to him. This somebody, in order to justify his natural impulse of disapprobation and annoyance, set his reason to work to establish good grounds for the blame which he desired to administer, partly to make the culprit uncomfortable, partly to preclude a repetition of the offence. The result is the coining of some moral maxim such as " Honesty is the best policy," or " A rolling stone gathers no moss," or " More haste less speed."

A man's reason habitually follows his impulses much as the feet of a hungry dog follows his nose, and the power of reason, when informed and impelled by a strong impulse, like the blaming impulse, is very remarkable. Reason can find the best possible justifications for the most outrageous conduct under the sun, and the best possible arguments for the most demonstrably fallacious beliefs. The belief, for instance, that " Honesty is the best policy " is still sincerely held and defended by men who would never dream of conducting their business activities for a moment upon such an assumption, experience having taught them that such a course would speedily bring them to ruin at the hands of their neighbours, who, though subscribing to the same belief with equal sincerity, are not accustomed to take their beliefs literally, or to regard them as a basis for action.

This activity of reason in building up ethical structures for the purpose of countenancing and as it were giving a purchase to the impulse to blame may be continually observed in practical life. If A has stood in a queue at a ticket office for five minutes, and observes B who has just come upon the scene edging his way into the queue in front of him, he feels a natural impulse to blame B for his confounded pushfulness. If B, possessing a turn for impudent logic, demands in answer to his protest why he has not as much right to indulge his immediate desire to get a ticket as A, the latter would probably support his protest by an appeal to some moral aphorism to the effect that people who come first should be first served, and would, if pressed further, indulge in some generally discursive remarks as to the effects of anti-social conduct such as B's, if emulated by others, upon society as a whole. " It would be a fine thing if every one were to go on like that," he would say.

Now it is important to point out that A did not first disapprove of B's conduct on rational grounds as anti-social, and likely if generally adopted to subvert the foundations of ordered society, and then administer a reproof upon the basis of his ratiocinations. He might allege that this was an accurate account of his mental workings, but his account would not be psychologically honest. Such a version in fact amounts to putting the cart before the horse. What usually happens in such cases is the occurrence of a strong feeling of resentment and annoyance coupled with an impulse to blame. This impulse is of a purely self-regarding character and does not involve any consideration of the possible effects upon the community at large of a universalization of the conduct reprehended. Such a consideration, bringing with it a condemnation on moral grounds of anti-social conduct, is the work of reason which rushes to the rescue of impulse when the latter is required to give an account of itself, and pretends that natural instinctive feelings are really the result of high moral consideration.

The same process which makes the man in the ticket queue talk about anti-social conduct, has, in a widely extended and glorified form, prompted the elaboration of ethical philosophies.

It is not difficult to see, for instance, in the moral sense theories a glorification of the impulse to blame, a glorification which elevates the impulse into a sort of universalised moral sense, in which form it immediately becomes a tremendous engine for the discomfiture of those who insist on the performance of actions to which we have an impulse to object. In the hands of writers like Kant, a double process of rationalization occurs. Not content with elevating the impulse to blame into a categorical imperative, thus endowing it with a status which enables it to wield complete authority over the world of action, he further supports it by giving it a metaphysical foundation, and linking it on to his theory of the Practical Reason.

Hedonistic and some Utilitarian theories have too often sought by destroying the canons of ordinary morality and insisting that pleasure is the only good, to glorify another impulse, the impulse to gratify bodily appetites. Where the moral sense theories are rationalizations of the self-denying and inhibitory impulses, the naturalistic and hedonistic theories rationalize the impulses to indulge.

The theories of the greater Utilitarians, Bentham and J. S. Mill, seem to have been rational embodiments of the meddling or political impulse, to which I shall come in the next chapter, rather than of the purely sensual impulses.

In this way we must regard the place of impulse in formulating our creeds as no less important than its function in dictating our actions. Reason is merely the machine which constructs the creed and plans the action. And in setting reason to justify impulse, impulse has the cunning to bribe reason to do the work, by fostering the delusion that reason is working autonomously, obeying no laws but its own and subject to no master. We have only to invert the simile used above to arrive at the real relationship between impulse and reason: impulse is the charioteer and reason draws the chariot, but the charioteer drives with a loose rein, giving his steeds their head, so that they may believe that it is they who select the course and dictate the pace.

The considerations set forth in this and the three foregoing sections will, I hope, sufficiently explain how the part played by impulse, both in prompting action and determining thought, has been so largely overlooked. I have been led perhaps in these sections to give undue emphasis to the importance of impulse, if only to redress the balance which has been so overweighted in favour of reason and of desire. I have also been led for the convenience of discussion to speak of impulse as if it were a distinct and isolated entity in the human make-up, and could be distinguished from and set over against reason as clearly as two individuals can be distinguished from each other. This of course is not the case. I do not mean to suggest either that impulse prompts all our actions, or that it determines all our beliefs; nor do I wish it to be supposed that impulse can be thought of as an independent entity, which does not shade into desire, and is not to some small extent informed by reason. All I wish to do is to establish the very great importance of impulse as a factor in human psychology. It remains to consider how far the life of impulse is at present provided for, and in what directions it can be developed, with a view to increasing the sum total of human happiness and freedom.

§ 4. Importance for Good Life of Liberation of Impulse

If the above outline of the psychology of impulse is correct, it will be realized how important a part impulse plays in our lives, and how necessary it is for Ethics to take the factor of impulse into account in estimating the conditions necessary for the production of the good life.

A general description of the place of impulse in the life of the modern civilized individual will be found in Mr. Bertrand Russell's " Principles of Social Reconstruction," Chapters I and VIII. It is not part of my purpose here to discuss or to recapitulate his theory, with which I largely agree, but only to consider its bearing upon Ethics. It will be sufficient therefore very briefly to indicate the attitude Mr. Russell adopts.

Impulse is the most important factor in the individual's make-up: it is the direct expression of his individuality, that which more than anything else distinguishes him from his fellows, and constitutes the peculiar essence of his personality.

It is the dynamic element in life which is constantly springing up anew in the individual; the principle of growth, and the source of change and progress. It is the driving force both of action and of thought: it impels men alike to satisfy their bodily needs at the table, and to gratify their intellectual curiosity by conducting recondite researches into the nature of infinity. It is in fact the expression of life itself.

In order therefore that the individual may live a full, rich and varied life, it is necessary that his impulses should have scope for expansion and development. The individual cannot be said properly to live unless his impulses are given free play, since it is only by following his impulses that he can develop his full nature and realize all that he has it in him to be.

If impulses are starved and thwarted therefore, two results may be said to follow. In the first place there is a general reduction in the vitality of the individual, which expresses itself in boredom and lack of interest. A life in which impulses are starved, or are subordinated to desires for distant ends, is a tiring and tedious affair, without joy and without zest, and the loss of vitality which results from an individuality at war within itself, renders the achievement of the end, in the interests of which the impulses have been suppressed, a source of little real satisfaction.

Both for communities and for individuals the suppression of impulse practised over a lengthy period saps vitality, and robs life of interest.

In the second place impulses which are thwarted are driven underground and either form the repressed complexes of whose danger psycho-analysts are never tired of warning us, or reappear in a form more undesirable, because perverted, than the original impulse.

Thus the healthy impulses of rivalry and contention which finds their proper outlet in games of strength and skill, when denied adequate expression, issue in the impulse of aggression which makes for war. This fact constitutes one of the reasons why the old who are precluded by sloth, feebleness or overeating from continuing the pursuits they followed at public schools, are more inclined to those aggressive and contentious policies which produce war, to a domineering love of power and authority, and to a pugnacious and irascible habit of mind, than the young, who are provided by the football field and the boxing ring with other outlets for this particular set of impulses.

Excessive discipline which looks with disfavour upon the impulse to self-expression, as rendering the individual incapable of fitting in to the uniform system required, frequently causes these impulses in men who are subject to it to transform themselves into impulses to cruelty and destruction.

In general either lack of vitality, or impulses which are oppressive or against life, will almost always result, if the spontaneous impulses are not able to find an outlet. The perpetual springing up of impulse may be compared to the flow of a river which, if it is artificially dammed, is driven underground or spreads over the countryside in the form of a foul and sullen marsh, and loses its brightness, its clearness and its energy.

Mr. Russell proceeds to show that the promptings of impulse are in fact thwarted to an unprecedented extent in the life of the modern civilized world.

In part this is the inevitable result of the highly organized industrial system under which a modern man obtains his livelihood. It is a system which consistently subordinates impulse to the desire to obtain a sufficient income; and the methods by which this income is obtained, instead of themselves affording scope for the expression of creative impulses, as is the case for instance with the work of the artist or the skilled craftsman, involve for the most part the rigorous suppression of all impulses that conflict with the necessity of concentrating attention upon some unending and monotonous process.

The business of getting a living, in fact, involves a constant process of immolating impulses, from the suppression in the early morning of the impulse to lie in bed, through the thwarting during the hours of work of the impulse to vary the uniformity of the articles which the demands of machine production require to be turned out in one unvarying mould, to the suppression of the impulse to sit up late at night in the interests of the desire to be in time at the factory next morning. The modern industrial system has divorced the business of production from the life of impulse, and the conditions under which a man's work afforded the chief scope for the play of his creative impulse have gone past recall.

Nor can men feel that this subordination of impulse is effected in the interests of their own desires. A man works under direction in order to achieve the ends not of himself but of others, and he becomes involuntarily subservient to purposes which he has no share in forming, and no interest, beyond the immediate interest of keeping his job, in achieving.

The growth of organization, especially in industry, is also inimical to the expression of impulse. Organization demands the subordination of the desires and impulses of a number of individual units to a general end. In the interests of this end all recalcitrant impulses which demand satisfaction for themselves at the expense of the general purpose in view must be rigorously suppressed. As civilization grows more complex, this is perhaps a necessary result, but it is one which unless counteracted by the enlargement of the scope of impulse in other directions, tends to produce that listlessness and lack of vitality which are salient characteristics of large and complex communities, and which have been remarked by historians to be at the root of the decay of societies such as that of ancient Rome.

Most important of all perhaps is the thwarting under modern conditions of what may be called the social or political impulse. All men have a strong desire to meddle with, and if possible to control, the lives of other individuals living in the same community. Most men have the well-being of the state deeply at heart, and wish to devote their energies and capacity to making the world more like the world they would wish to see. The political impulse is as strong as any of the great impulses which all men possess in common, and expresses itself in the desire of the individual to take hold, in however small a degree, of the forces that control society. The individual wishes to feel that he counts, that his views matter, and in face of the enormously complex organism of the modern state he cannot but feel that he does not count: his efforts to take hold are futile.

I will deal in more detail with this subject in the next chapter.

The conclusion would seem to be that it is necessary, if we wish to restore joy and vitality to life, to pay more attention to the demands of impulse, and to devise conditions under which these demands can be more adequately met. An important distinction, however, should be drawn between two classes of impulses, of which the former requires encouraging, while the latter already receives encouragement to the detriment of happiness and freedom in the world. These are the class of creative impulses and the class of possessive impulses respectively.

"Some of our actions," says Mr. Russell, "are devoted to creating what would not otherwise exist, others are directed to acquiring or retaining what exists already. The typical creative impulse is that of the artist : the typical possessive impulse is that of property." Now the best life " is that in which creative impulses play the largest part and possessive impulses the smallest." Our theory therefore is not one which tells us that all impulses are to be encouraged and indulged merely because they are impulses. Some impulses, the creative ones, are to be encouraged at the expense of the others.

And for this distinction there is a very obvious reason. The creative impulses can be encouraged and indulged to an unlimited extent without interfering with the impulses of others. When the creative impulse of the artist produces a picture, the result does not impede the production of other artists, but rather acts as a stimulus to activity, by challenging their emulation. The possessive impulse, however, which leads a man to acquire and retain a large fortune can only be gratified by the deprivation of others.

Creative impulses issue as a rule in the production of things which may be enjoyed by an indefinite number of people. A symphony or a poem is like the air, the country, or the sea in this, that the fact of its being enjoyed by any number of people, however great, is no obstacle to its enjoyment by others. The possessive impulses on the other hand, instead of increasing the possibilities of enjoyment, limit them by confining them to the possessor and his friends. It is easy to see how the indulgence of the possessive impulses leads to strife and conflict, whereas creative impulses may be harmoniously developed to an indefinite extent.

Modern societies, however, besides penalizing the creative impulses, as we have seen above, by necessarily subordinating them to desires for economic ends, are constituted in such a way as to place an undue value upon the activities of the possessive impulses.

It is possible to instance important social institutions such as education, marriage and religion which, though essentially creative in origin, have become bulwarks for the maintenance of the *status quo*, and for guaranteeing the continued enjoyment of the possessive impulses of those who control them.

We live under a system which, though paying lip service to the religion of Christ, who waged unceasing war upon the possessive impulses—" Take no thought, saying, what shall we eat ? or What shall we drink, or Wherewithal shall we be clothed ? "—creates a scale of values which counts only the achievements of the possessive impulses, by making income and property the chief criterion of importance and success. We are governed by the " stomach and pocket " point of view ; the impulses that demand beauty and spaciousness and leisure, spaciousness for romance and leisure for creation, being brushed aside as incompatible with the all important business of getting on, which being interpreted means the acquisition of the means for increasing our material possessions.

The possessive impulses are not a direct expression of the principle of growth ; they are the outcome of what is static and conservative in human nature, rather than of what is dynamic and changing. In those who are old the possessive impulses have achieved an almost complete victory over their inconvenient creative brethren, and it is for this reason that our institutions, which are the embodiment and expression of the ideals of the old, aim at perpetuating possession by setting upon it the seal of security and respectability.

Impulses can be changed and diverted by circumstance, education and environment. Almost every boy has an impulse towards cruelty ; he wishes to pull the wings off flies, to stick pins through the bodies of butterflies, and to destroy birds' nests for the mere pleasure which these activities bring him. By education which is devoted to developing contrary impulses, the impulse to cruelty may be transformed into one of kindness and fellow-feeling towards other sentient creatures. The reverse process is alleged by some to occur in the case of surgeons, who having begun to practise vivisection in the interests of scientific knowledge, have continued it for its own sake, not having perceived its effect of unwittingly developing their hitherto latent impulse towards cruelty.

It should be part of the study of practical Ethics to consider the conditions which are most favourable to the growth of creative impulses, and to value political and social institutions in proportion as they encourage them or provide scope for their development. The supreme principle both in politics and in private life should, according to Mr. Russell, be " to promote all that is creative, and so to diminish the impulses and desires that centre round possession."

§ 5. Possible Objections to Theory of Impulse

I have outlined in brief, expanded and adapted this theory of Mr. Russell's as to the function of impulse because it appears to me to have an important bearing upon the problems of Ethics. It also provides a good example of the method which should, I think, be pursued by students of empirical Ethics. Yet I am aware that it may be termed unphilosophical in appearance and presentation, and that it is perhaps open to a series of formal objections on philosophical grounds.

Although the theory does not pretend to the logical completeness of the *a priori* systems we considered earlier, and is indeed based on the supposition that both the method and conclusions of those theories are ill adapted to deal with the multifarious diversity of human psychology, it is important that it should be able to provide a defence for itself against philosophical attack.

The main objection that can, I think, be brought against it is that it provides no adequate means for discriminating those impulses which it is desired to express from those which should be kept under.

We have seen that the theory does not advocate the indiscriminate indulgence of all impulses, concentrating rather on the encouragement of creative impulses, nor do I think that the proposition that all impulses should be indulged can seriously be entertained as an Ethical maxim. Plato draws in the Republic a terrifying picture of the life of the man who is completely at the mercy of every passing impulse. He divides the soul into three parts, the reasoning part, the spirited part, and the part that is composed of impulse and desire, and conceives of three different kinds of lives that can be lived, according as one part or another is given the predominance.

The desiring part of the soul is graphically compared to a many-headed monster, who, by demanding constant satisfaction for his insatiable appetites, makes the life of the "desiring man" a miserable slavery to the whims of his unchecked passions. Such a life is without unity or purpose; it is a mere succession of desires which confer only a momentary pleasure when sated, and grow in imperiousness when disappointed. Plato concludes that the soul can only be at peace within itself, and that man's lives can in consequence only attain to a degree of unity and tranquillity, when the desiring part of the soul is in subjection to the reasoning part.

We have seen reason above to doubt this particular conclusion, which overlooks the facts, first that reason must in a very real sense always be the servant of desire, and second that recalcitrant desires and impulses which fail to fit in with the general scheme of life pursued by the individual can only be checked, not by reason, but by other impulses and desires.

There can, however, be no question as to the justice of Plato's indictment of the life of unbridled desire. We may agree with Oscar Wilde that the only way to get rid of a temptation is to yield to it, on a question of fact, but as a question of expediency we know that such a course only results in substituting another desire for the one we have sated.

We are driven, therefore, to the conclusion that even when attempting to enrich and develop the life of impulse, we must exercise a rigid censorship over certain impulses in the interests of others.

On what principle is this to be done? A hint as to where we are to look for the answer is to be found in the Ethics of Aristotle. A sketch of the place of desire and will in Aristotle's theory of Ethics was given in Chapter II, but it will be convenient here briefly to recapitulate his conclusions. Aristotle describes with the same kind of disapproval as

Plato, the life of the man who is a prey to his own conflicting desires and impulses. These desires and impulses are for the most part blind and irresponsible. In demanding satisfaction for themselves, they take no heed for the good of the individual as a whole, and would have him obey their dictates irrespective of the resultant loss to the whole, which includes the deprivation of other desires.

Besides these irresponsible desires and impulses, however, Aristotle recognizes a further desire which he calls the desire for the good of the whole. This desire for the good of the whole is by some identified with what we will call, and by others is thought of as being, that desire which is able to enlist the will in its service. We have seen above that it is misleading to speak of any desire as rational, in the sense that it can be said to spring from rational reflection, or can give a rational account of its origin, or a rational justification for obtaining its fulfilment. At the same time it is possible to speak of one desire as being more rational than another, in the sense that a life devoted to the attainment of its end is more likely to bring real satisfaction and enjoyment than the momentary or illusory satisfaction which waits on the fulfilment of the so-called irrational desires.

A rational desire is thus one which in the interests of general satisfaction it is worth while to pursue : it is a better investment than an irrational one. Now it is clear that what Aristotle calls the desire for the good of the whole is a rational desire in this sense. It is obvious that if we can determine what the good of the whole is, we are more likely to gain in satisfaction by pursuing it, than we are by yielding to a crop of indiscriminate desires and impulses, changing and repeating themselves from day to day, whose satisfaction is probably detrimental to what we call our real good.

In the interests of the good of the whole then, the good, or, as Aristotle tends to call him, " the happy " or sometimes " the prudent man," will use his will to police and discipline the indiscriminate desires and impulses, reducing them to order, and permitting them only that amount of satisfaction which is compatible with the good of the whole. They will be dovetailed into one another : compromises will be made : and the line of action that is actually pursued will often be a resultant of a number of desires none of which it actually represents.

The trouble about this account is that although it is easy enough on paper to define the good of the whole, establishing it by the irrefutable methods of *a priori* reasoning as pleasure, virtue, aesthetic enjoyment, or what not (Aristotle himself identified it with the undisturbed contemplation of certain unchangeable entities of a mixed mathematical and theological character), this good of the whole is not in practice easy to determine.

We may pursue an ideal, but we can never affirm that its attainment will be good for us. No general aim or ambition is constant : it changes as we change and recedes as we approach ; nor is it possible as a rule to state it even to ourselves in definite terms.

What we can do, however, is to pursue certain definite purposes or groups of purposes. They may be of a provisional character : they may not be comprehensive : and their apparent desirability may be illusory : but if steadfastly approached they do give an aim and unity to our otherwise masterless lives, and incidentally they provide a stick with which to beat unruly impulses. A man is free only when he does so govern his life according to some such dominant purpose, and it is in the interest of such a purpose that he will use his will to check impulses that conflict with it.

Two provisos must, however, be carefully kept in mind.

In the first place the purpose must be voluntarily subscribed to on the part of the individual, and the use of will to check conflicting impulses in the interest of the dominant purpose must also be voluntary. Will is too often used to check impulses in order to serve the purposes of others, and the occasions on which impulses are repressed are too often forced upon the individual by outside pressure instead of being voluntarily chosen. Economic necessity is the most frequent occasion of the use of will to repress impulses which might endanger the all important business of earning a living. The forces of convention and public opinion are often effective, especially among women, in the strangling of impulses whose indulgence might be derogatory to the reputation or good name of the individual.

The repression of impulses by will in such cases is not freely chosen ; it is forced upon the individual from without, and the slavery to will which is set in motion by outside pressure is as inimical to real freedom as the slavery to impulse and desire which the will is designed to check. It is desirable not that a man should always indulge his impulses, but that he should always be able to indulge them if he wants to.

In the second place it should be borne in mind that the repression of impulse by will, even in cases freely chosen by the individual, is not really desirable, and should be minimized as far as possible. Will should be used externally to overcome obstacles to the fulfilment of impulse, rather than internally to check impulses. The frequent suppression of impulse is the sign of an individual at war within himself. If constantly practised it dries up the springs of energy and vitality, and produces a barren and listless life. It is often more desirable to take risks through the following of impulse than to play for safety by repressing the impulse to new and adventurous courses. People are too inclined to let their little wisdoms stifle their big impulses, and to seek consolation by regarding themselves as moral, rational, or what not, for doing it. Life may be regarded as a discipline or as an opportunity, according as we tend to repress or to indulge our impulses. In the first case we shall be oppressed by the continual fear of mistakes, in the second we shall be inspired by the glorious possibilities of experiment.

"A life governed by purposes and desires, to the exclusion of impulse, is a tiring life," says Mr. Russell: "it exhausts vitality and leaves a man, in the end, indifferent to the very purposes he has been trying to achieve."

Such a life may be compared to the common practice of the man who spends his youth and middle age repressing his impulses in saving and scraping to acquire the means to retire and travel in his old age, only to find that in the process of acquiring the money he has lost the taste for travelling.

In stating therefore that as a necessary condition of a free and happy life, impulses which conflict with a dominant purpose or set of purposes must frequently be suppressed, I do not mean to imply that the word "must" has any binding force, comparable to that usually attached to the moral "ought." I mean that as a matter of empirical fact, it is found that greater satisfaction attends a life which achieves a measure of unity from the pursuit of certain definite purposes, in the interests of which conflicting impulses are suppressed, than a life which is the slave of passing whims, and is supported by no central unity or principle of growth. A man ascending a Sussex down from time to time experiences an impulse to turn and look back upon the gradually expanding view. If he is wise he will as a rule suppress the impulse in order that when he reaches the top, the full view may burst upon him with a freshness undiminished by previous acquaintance with a merely partial aspect. It is in incidents of this kind that we see the desirability of suppressing certain impulses in the interests of a more important impulse, whose fruition would be impaired by the premature indulgence of its forerunners.

I have thought it necessary to mention cases of this kind through fear, had I omitted them, of conveying the impression that the Ethical life as I conceived it was a process of simply doing what one wanted to.

It is of course not so simple as that: inhibition is frequently necessary; we must economize our wants, and concentrate on some to the exclusion of others, simply because it is humanly impossible to satisfy all.

Morality: the Substitute of the Old for the Impulses of the Young

But the necessity of inhibition, control and self-discipline has been stressed too often in the past to require elaboration here. Moralists have unduly weighed the scales against impulse, and to redress the balance our emphasis must be placed on the other side. It is not the desirability of suppressing impulse that requires stressing, the moralists will see to that: it is the desirability of encouraging it.

I am well aware how far removed are the suggestions I have put forward from the traditional systems which have hitherto held the field in Ethics. I do not think, however, that this consideration in itself need trouble us, or cause suspicions as to the soundness of our analysis. For reasons already enumerated, there has been a kind of conspiracy on the part of philosophers to ignore the claims of impulse. It is a conspiracy in which the world of common sense has been only too ready to participate. The moral maxims and precepts of any age are usually the expression of the wisdom of its older men. They are the means by which the old lay down rules of guidance for the young. They draw their inspiration not only from the impulse to blame, of which we already have spoken, as the substructure which underlies and informs most moral codes, but from the subconscious working of the principle of sour grapes in those who, no longer capable of enjoying the sweets of life, would accordingly deny them to those who are.

" Old men give young men good advice, no longer being able to give them bad examples," wrote Wycherly. As regards women, the dog-in-the-manger attitude of older members of the sex towards pleasures from which they are themselves debarred by timidity or age is notorious. The Greek doctrine of self-expression has filtered down to us through centuries of Roman Stoicism and English Puritanism, which forbid with envy lurking at their hearts—the envy of the incomplete man for him who dares express himself. This morality which is founded on fear finds its extreme expression in prudery. Prudery is the old woman's caricature of morality. It is the fig leaf of the imagination.

Thus it comes about that the old, who have in the past set the standard of behaviour for the young, have combined to paint for their edification a picture of a gloomy and treacherous world in which the young rush to destruction, until they learn to know better; a destruction which can effectually be averted only by following the inhibitory advice of those who have learned to know better. The young may not, it seems, judging from the example of and spectacle of their elders, achieve any positive joy or freedom by following this advice, but they can at least live safely and avoid catastrophe.

It is envy of the capacities of the young which has largely inspired the doctrine of original sin, a doctrine which has had much to do with the general distrust of impulse. It is because the heart of man has been held to be at bottom wicked, that the practice of listening to its promptings has been so universally discouraged. In the case of children who are subject to a greater degree than adults to the promptings of impulse uninformed by reason, the results of this pernicious doctrine are most clearly manifest. It is only to-day that we are beginning to outgrow the Victorian attitude to children as vessels of wrath and imps of Satan, whose main function in the world is to give grown-ups an opportunity first to prepare hot water for them to fall into, and then to scold them for falling into it.

The distrust of impulse is thus at bottom a doctrine of despair in human nature. It assumes that if human nature is to have its way it must necessarily go to the devil. Yet if we are to increase the happiness and freedom in the world, if we are to believe in the possibility of a fuller and richer life for man, we must base our Ethics on an attitude of hope and trust. We must believe that impulse instead of being an emanation of our lower nature to be rigorously held in check by reason, is the source of our greatest good, just as it may contain the seeds of our greatest evil. And we must also believe that if human nature is allowed to have its head, the impulses to good will triumph over the impulses to evil. The following passage from Shaw's pamphlet, "The Sanity of Art," finely expresses the grounds for our faith in the sanity of impulse : " If the heart of man is deceitful above all things and desperately wicked, then truly the man who allows himself to be guided by his passions must needs be a scoundrel. . . . But how if the youth thrown helpless on his passions found that honesty, that self-respect, that hatred of cruelty and injustice, that the desire for soundness and health and efficiency, were master passions : nay that their excess is so dangerous to youth that it is part of the wisdom of age to say to the young : ' Be not righteous overmuch : why shouldst thou destroy thyself ? ' "

CHAPTER VI

THE PLACE OF IMPULSE IN POLITICS AND SOCIETY

§ 1. Relation between Ethics and Politics

THE closeness of the relation between Ethics and Politics does not need demonstration. Ethics is concerned with the good of the individual, politics with the good of the State: but the State is in fact an accumulation of individuals, so that the good of the State really means the good of the individuals who compose it. This statement remains accurate, even if we concede the truth of the view of many political philosophers that the State has a kind of secondary or independent existence of its own, apart from the individuals in it. Politics therefore is that brand of Philosophy which considers the good of the individual as a member of a community, while Ethics considers the good of the individual as an isolated entity.

This near relation between Ethics and Politics was fully realized by the Greeks. We have already had occasion to note the belief of Greek philosophers that there was one, and only one Good which it was the business of Ethical philosophers to discover. It followed from this conception of the one Good, that there was one good life which all men, or at any rate most men, ought to lead, namely, the life which consisted in the pursuit of the one Good. It is the business therefore of the lawgivers to pass such laws as will promote the one good life among the citizens. If the laws are sufficiently good, the mere practice of obedience to them on the part of the citizens will be sufficient to ensure their living the good life.

(The fact that the lawgiver himself was conceived of as

having a different good life from that of the ordinary citizen, a life that consisted mainly in contemplation, need not detain us here.)

While the Ethical philosopher is concerned therefore to define the good life for the individual, it is the business of the Political philosopher to help him to live it. Now the good life can only be lived by individuals whose natures are fully developed. Man is a political and social animal. He cannot be moral all by himself, or live the good life on a desert island: for the good life, as conceived by the Greeks, is a full, rich, free life providing for the expression of every part of our nature, and the development of all our tastes and talents. That is why the good life can only be lived in society, for it is only in society that a man attains to his true nature, and to that complete development of all his faculties without which he is not truly a man. It is only through intercourse with his fellows that he can realize all that he has it in him to be. The State or society was therefore for the Greeks an indispensable adjunct to the good life, and the Ethical philosopher must of necessity embrace the good of the State in his purview, when writing out his prescription for the good of the individual.

This theory did not stop with the Greeks. In the hands of German philosophers like Kant and Hegel it was developed and transformed until the notion that society, or the State, was an indispensable condition of the good life for the individual, grew into the conception that the individual owed a debt of gratitude to the State for performing this beneficial work of developing his personality. Furthermore the State, being representative of all the individuals in it, came to be regarded as a kind of glorified expression of their real selves, indissolubly linked with them by a mysterious bond of community, and representative of all that was highest in their natures. In this conception a fresh ground was found for unquestioning obedience to the State, and the good life for the individual came to consist in sacrifice and discipline for the State's sake.

I have thought it desirable briefly to sketch the results arrived at by this school, in order to show that the intimacy of the bond between Ethics and Politics is established from whatever side we approach the subject, and so to avoid the accusation of undue trespassing. It is not, however, part of our task to follow the political speculations of Greek and German philosophers further. Our method of approach to the subject will be somewhat different.

As a result of the Liberal and individualist thinking of the nineteenth century, we have largely abandoned the idea that there is one good life for all men which ought to be universally followed irrespective of individual idiosyncrasy: we have come to hold, on the contrary, that it is not the business of anybody, even though he be a lawgiver, or an Ethical philosopher, to prescribe for others the sort of life which they ought to lead. We believe that different people ought to lead different lives and, with occasional lapses in war time, we believe that they should be permitted to live their own lives without interference, provided that their doing so does not interfere with the good lives of others.

It is not therefore in our view the business of the politician or the lawgiver to preach or prescribe codes of morals for the citizens. But the State is in theory only an organization for securing human happiness, whatever it may be in practice, and we must accordingly concede to the politician that concern with the happiness of individuals that we deny him with regard to their morals.

But happiness is generally held to be unattainable without freedom, and as we are taking as an example for our experiment in the methods of empirical Ethics, the investigation and encouragement of those impulses which make for happiness and freedom, we are bound to consider how these impulses fare at the hands of society. We have tried to show in the last chapter that the life of impulse is intimately bound up with human happiness and freedom ; and since it is the object of the lawgiver to promote happiness and freedom, it would seem to be his business to make provision for the life of impulse, and the business of the student of empirical Ethics to consider how far he does so.

I propose therefore to proceed to consider in what ways the necessary relationship between Ethics and Politics expresses itself in practice, and what conditions a political system should necessarily fulfil if it is to make adequate provision for the expression of impulse.

In so doing it will not be necessary to treat definitely of any existing political organization ; it will be sufficient to indicate generally the type of institution which is favourable to the life of impulse, and the type of institution most inimical to it.

§ 2. Forms of the Relation

I think it is possible to distinguish four different ways in which the necessary relation between Ethics and Politics expresses itself. I propose to consider these ways in some little detail because our consideration of them will throw much light on the part played by impulse in social and political life. In the first two forms of this relation the rôle played by Politics is that merely of a background to the good life, or as I prefer to call it for the purposes of this discussion, the fuller life of impulse; the third exhibits political or social activity as being in itself an important expression of the life of impulse; the fourth requires that Politics shall provide an outlet for the creative impulse in the sphere of work.

The State as the Background of the Good Life

I. The first form of the relation is sufficiently obvious. However we conceive of the good life, it cannot be lived without order and security. It is the business of the State, and it is therefore one of the objects of Politics to enforce order and to ensure security.

This result is accomplished by the State in two ways. It protects the individual by the law and its instrument the police force from physical violence, and it acts as a check, or should do so, upon the blind operations of economic force.

The Necessity of Security

(a) Protection from physical violence is an essential condition of the pursuit of the good life. Most men are subject to an impulse to do harm to those whom they happen to dislike, or whom they believe to have injured them. Though most of us are able, as the result of the traditions and habits of civilized life, to subdue such impulses, yet there exists in every society a small number of anti-social individuals, who, whether as a means of avenging a private spite, or as a method of gaining their livelihood, would form the practice of preying upon their neighbours unless deterred by fear of the law. That the veneer of civilization which veils the primitive man in all of us is of the thinnest, is sufficiently evidenced by the comparatively recent survival of duelling, and the satisfaction experienced by most men in witnessing a bull fight or a boxing exhibition. To safeguard individual security, and to establish some method of settling disputes other than the resort to violence is one of the chief functions of the State, and it is to the desire for such a safeguard that we may attribute one of the chief causes which have predisposed men to live in societies.

As Plato puts it in the Republic, every man in a state of nature desires to do injustice to his fellows; finding, however, that such a state of existence was intolerable, people decided to live in societies, thereby surrendering their right to do injustice to their fellows, on condition that they were guaranteed a similar immunity from the desires of others. And although it is untrue that men ever made a definite contract to live in society on these terms, the bargain is nevertheless implied in all our social arrangements. Translating Plato into modern language we may say that in the interests of order and security we restrain our impulse to vent our justifiable annoyance on the person of a red-haired man who wears a straw hat, on condition that he exercises a similar restraint with regard to our pernicious habit of smelling of eucalyptus.

Order and security do not in themselves form a part of the good life, but they are the indispensable background of it, the permanent condition of the possibility of there being a good life. We may regard the good as intellectual contemplation or the pursuit of knowledge; but the philosopher cannot philosophize if he is in constant danger of having his throat cut. We may regard it as social service and the betterment of the lives of others; but the philanthropist cannot philanthropize if his stomach craves for a meal and a burglar has stolen his loose cash. The good man, it has been said, can be happy on the rack. This statement may have been true provided he was a very good man, and it was a very bad rack; but generally speaking the spectacle of any philosopher with the toothache is sufficient to demonstrate the necessity of immunity from the cruder forms of physical want or discomfort, before we can indulge in the luxury of morals, or the cultivation of the intellect.

The security therefore which is necessary for the possibility of Ethics can be provided by the State and only by the State. In all the ages of the world, moral, intellectual or aesthetic advance has become possible only when the politician sufficiently performed his function of guaranteeing the necessary background of the lives of the reformer, the scholar, and the artist. A certain degree of leisure and spaciousness is required before we can afford the time or the energy to pursue the good. It is only when men have lived for a considerable period under conditions which have freed them from the grosser cares of life that they have been disposed to produce good and beautiful works. These conditions are security, freedom, and a sense of self-respect, and they can be attained for men as a whole only as the result of good government.

Blindness of Economic Law

(*b*) The importance of the economic factor in the good life is not less than freedom from physical violence, and is almost as directly the concern of the State. Economic freedom, like security from violence, is not necessarily a constituent part of morality or of happiness, but it is to an equal degree the indispensable condition of the pursuit of the one or the achievement of the other. It is a commonplace that wealth does not make men happy : it is equally true that they cannot be happy, and we may add that they cannot be moral, without at least a competency. That part of morality for instance which consists of respect for private property is meaningless to a man with a starving wife and children, who sees the opportunity of stealing a leg of mutton from a butcher's shop ; nor is it reasonable to expect a hungry person to tell the truth, when by a secure lie he can obtain a square meal.

Thus the practice of virtue is a luxury dependent upon the possession of a sufficient income ; and many thinkers have accordingly regarded it as lying within the State's function to assure a competency to each of its members irrespective of the value of their services. Hence arise schemes for providing an equal income for all men whatever work they perform ; hence Anarchist and Communist theories which insist that all men should receive in accordance with their needs instead of being as at present paid in proportion to their deserts, their good fortune, their push or their unscrupulousness.

It is not possible here to enter into a discussion as to the merits of these theories, even if they can be regarded as practicable. Such a discussion belongs more properly to the realm of political theory. It is important, however, to note that they have an ethical basis and are propounded with an ethical object. They say in effect, " Since it is impossible to live the good life unless men are economically secure, it is the business of Politics to see that men are economically secure." If these theories are right, they point us once more to the conclusion that it is the business of Politics to provide the background of Ethics.

There is another respect in which the interference of the State in economic matters is necessary for the good life. Under modern conditions the economic action of small groups of men produces an enormous effect upon the lives and welfare of others. As a rule this effect is neither foreseen nor intended. Hence arises the so-called " blindness " of economic action. Economic action is blind in the sense that it aims only at the good of a small group of people without considering the rest, whereas political action aims, or should aim, at the good of the community as a whole. It is the function of the State therefore to check the blind results of the economic action of a few people upon the lives and happiness of the citizens as a whole. If for example a rumour is spread to the effect that a certain bank is likely to fail, the effect is an immediate rush on the part of all the clients of the bank to withdraw their money before the threatened collapse takes place. The inevitable result is the failure of the bank, a result which nobody either willed or intended, but which was on the contrary the exact negation of the hopes and wishes of everybody concerned. It is results of this kind which are produced by the blind effects of economic law, and the abandonment of the *laissez faire* theories of the nineteenth century, as evidenced by the passing of the Factory Acts, the more recent measures against profiteering and the control of food prices, show that the function of the State in checking such results is sufficiently realized.

But in assuming this function for the State, Politics is once again acting as the handmaiden of Ethics. It is because the blind results of economic action are inimical to the pursuit of the good life, that it is admitted to be the business of the State to check them.

The art of Politics therefore must be sufficiently understood and efficiently practised not as a part of Ethics, but as an indispensable condition of the possibility of there being Ethics.

Obligation of Politics to Needs of Impulse

II. It is necessary to bring the function of Politics, in guaranteeing the background of the good life, into more explicit connection with the position taken up in the last chapter as to the importance of the life of impulse.

If one of the means to the good life is the fuller expression of impulses and in particular of the creative impulses, it will be necessary for politics to establish the conditions most favourable for this expression. Impulses, as we have already noticed, can be changed by environment: they can be given new directions, and fresh scope; impulses that make for life can be developed by encouragement; impulses that make for death or strife can be sublimated or directed into more beneficial channels.

It is the business of politics to discover the soil most suitable for the growth and expression of the creative impulses, and to remove the incentives which at present exist for the exclusive expression of the possessive impulses.

It is not possible here to work out in detail how this could be done; but it is sufficiently obvious that many institutions, which have at present become the chief stronghold of the possessive impulses, might be transformed by Politics into what is creative.

In the institution of marriage, for example, the economic dependence of women and the rigidity of the divorce laws put a premium upon possession, the former establishing the claim to possession on the part of the husband who provides a livelihood, the latter making it impossible for the wife to resist the claim short of actual crime or cruelty on the part of the husband. Thus the higher creative aspects of marriage are thrust into the background by the sense of possession, which precludes that freedom which is the necessary condition of the nobler forms of human intercourse.

In religion God is still for most men a kind of tribal or national possession of reliable patriotic sympathies, made by man in his own image to supply a need of human nature, and to invest the intolerable insignificance of the individual's life with the importance that comes from the belief in an all-powerful being, caring for and interested in his welfare. The religious insight of individuals, which is the source of all advance in moral and spiritual conceptions, is unable to find an outlet within the narrow and inelastic boundaries of the creeds that tell us of this semi-human god.

Education has been devoted to perpetuating the traditions and handing on the possessions of the past, rather than to encouraging the creative vision which is to mould the future. It is designed to fill the pupil's mind with dead and unassimilated facts, rather than to assist him to strike out sparks of inspiration from his own soul : it has taught him what to think rather than how to think.

By changing the spirit of institutions it is possible to make them stimulate the expression of impulses which they now suppress. If the life of impulse is good and ought to be encouraged, it rests with the art of Politics so to mould our institutions that they make adequate provision for its encouragement.

Importance of Political Impulse

III. Of all the impulses which it is desired to encourage, the political or social impulse is perhaps the most important, as it is certainly the most commonly neglected. When Mill made the test of right and wrong in conduct, the promotion of the greatest happiness of the greatest number, his criterion was not so much at odds with the facts of human psychology as has sometimes been thought. For oddly enough people do care intensely about the happiness and welfare of others. And because it is true of almost all men that they do care about the well-being of their fellows, they desire vaguely to influence the lives of others and to make the world a better place.

The flood of Utopias, which has inundated the bookstalls, is only the literary expression of this fundamental impulse of all of us to induce other people to lead the kind of lives which we think they ought to lead. It is this impulse which I have called the political or social impulse, and for its outlet and recognition the structure of the modern world makes little provision. It is because people are unable to express themselves politically, to influence the lives of men, and to feel that they count in public affairs, that they come to seem to others, and in the course of time to themselves, self-centred and cynical, with no interests outside the circles of family and business, within which their immediate activities lie. Thus the political impulse is thought not to exist, where in most men it has once existed and has become atrophied. The suppression of this impulse, which is the fault neither of individuals nor of society as a whole, reacts unfavourably upon the good life in two ways. If we are able to establish that these reactions are in fact harmful to the individual, we shall be in a position to ask that politics should make more adequate provision for the expression of this political impulse than it has done in the past.

Thwarting of the Political Impulse

(*a*) Whether the political or social impulse, as I have termed it, is or is not fundamental in human nature I do not know. The question is one for the biologists to answer. It is sufficient that it is of long standing, its strength and persistence arising from the circumstance that man is a political and social being who has lived for the past five hundred generations in society. And since the welfare or misfortune of society produce an undeniable effect for good or ill upon the individual, it is only natural to put the matter on its lowest ground, that the individual should care enormously about the well-being of society, that is, of the other people who belong to society besides himself.

Thus it comes about that most of us have the *salus populi* deeply at heart, and that people do, in spite of all appearances to the contrary, bother themselves about the happiness and welfare of others, especially of those others who happen to be poor. The widespread interest in Politics in the narrowly accepted sense of the word, Politics being professedly concerned with the good of society as a whole, is only one expression of this deep-seated impulse.

It follows from this general interest in the lives and

welfare of others, that the individual desires to influence and if possible to control their development. It is not enough to be interested in the " well-being of the people " if you cannot lift a finger to change their lot for good or for ill, if you are powerless to meddle with their lives, or to set before them your own particular ideals of how life ought to be lived. Hence arises the almost universal desire for some sort of influence or control, however limited, in the affairs of the State. Men wish to feel somehow that they count, that their thoughts and actions matter, and that it is not beyond the bounds of possibility that some one of their thoughts or actions might really influence the State, and through the State the lives of others.

In certain cases this desire to count may simply be due to the impulse for self-assertion, and the number of such cases no doubt appears to be on the increase : sometimes it is based on mixed motives, the desire for notoriety and the desire to influence and control the lives of others being blended : more usually, however, it springs directly from the political impulse, which makes us desire weight in the councils of our society in order that we may counsel it for what we believe to be its good.

Whatever be the mainspring of the feeling, the impulse to take hold somehow or somewhere is, broadly speaking, universal. Yet this impulse must, under modern conditions, inevitably be thwarted. So vast are the forces at work in society, so complex and elaborate the structure of Government, and so intricate and difficult to disentangle the different strands that condition events, that so far from controlling them men are unable even to understand them. In face of the complex organism of society the individual feels helpless and impotent. Events which occur seem to be not so much the result of human will and effort, as of the interplay of blind and uncontrollable forces whose genesis escapes detection, and whose object, if any, is shrouded in mystery. Men are driven more and more to that interpretation of phenomena with which Mr. Hardy's novels have made us familiar, to the notion of a blind, unthinking Thing, which conditions the march of events without apparent design or will, which furthers human efforts without purpose and thwarts them without malignity ; a Thing before whose power man's endeavour is powerless, or if it succeeds, successful by chance and not by intrinsic merit.

And this conception is thrust upon men not through an intellectual adhesion to the doctrines of determinism, nor from any spiritual flirting with fatalism, but simply from the spectacle of a world mechanism so vast that the individual man seems powerless to modify its workings or to mould its ends. It is this notion of a canvas too big for human designs that seems to have inspired Mr. Keynes' famous comment on the working of the forces that went to produce the Peace Treaty: " One felt most strongly the impression described by Tolstoy in War and Peace, or by Hardy in the Dynasts, of events marching on to their fated conclusion uninfluenced and unaffected by the cerebrations of Statesmen in Council."

It is the size of the machine which thwarts the individual's impulse to take hold, to feel that his opinions count, and that his actions can be made to matter, and not any necessary characteristic of Politics which makes them unamenable to human control.

Apathy resulting from Size of Modern State

As a result of this feeling of impotence, the impulse to politics either perishes from inanition, or becomes diverted into untoward channels whose outlets would be humorous if they were not pathetic. Those whose impulse seeks an emotional rather than an intellectual outlet, whose hearts are, in common parlance, better than their heads, seek in social work and meddling with the lives of the poor that satisfaction which they fail to find in real political activity. The respect which their superior culture, wealth and manners obtain for them amongst the lower classes, create the fiction that here at last is to be found that sphere of influence in which they may mould the lives of others after the ideals approved by themselves. Thus the political impulse finds its vent in investigating the habits of the poor, cataloguing their deficiencies, stigmatizing their wastefulness, and distributing coal and blankets to mitigate the more acute forms of distress among the so-called deserving.

Those whose characteristics are pre-eminently intellectual, whose heads are better than their hearts, finding that the magnitude and impersonality of the forces that govern society deny their talents their natural scope in the control and improvement of the lives of others, sink into that spirit of soured cynicism, satirical flippancy, and political apathy which is so characteristic of the intelligentsias of the modern world.

They cry sour grapes at politics, stigmatize it as a dirty game in which the stakes are personal ambition instead of the welfare of the community and retire, as did the Russian intellectuals in the last years of the Tsardom, to dilettantism, introspection, the cultivation of their souls, and the pursuit of art for art's sake.

Such a picture as that drawn in Shaw's " Heartbreak House " of the best brains in the country, refusing to interest themselves in politics, and centring their lives round the interplay of personal relations and of sexual intrigue, is a successful attempt to crystallize in the presentation of a few individuals the withering effects upon the intellectuals produced by the failure of the political impulse to find its true outlet. " A Fantasia in the Russian Manner " is the title of the play, and restlessness, hysteria and futility are shown to be the Nemesis that waits on those who endeavour to find in the world of personal relations a substitute for the life of politics and affairs, which they have discarded in disgust. The weariness of such pursuits and their inadequacy as a dominating purpose for men of intelligence, is brought out by comparison in an account by Mr. Ransome of the effect upon a modern Russian audience of a Tchekov play written under the Tsardom and produced under the Bolshevik régime.

" Tchekov's irony places before us wasted lives, hopelessness, exaggerated interest in personalities, vain strugglings after some better outlet for the expression of selves not worth expressing.

" That play, acted to-day, seemed as remote as a play of the old régime in France would have seemed five years ago. A gulf seemed to have passed. The play had become a play of historical interest; the life it represented had gone for ever. People in Russia no longer have time for private lives of such a character. Such people no longer exist; some of them have been swept into the flood-tide of revolution, and are working as they never hoped to have the chance to work; others, less generous, have been broken and thrown aside. The revolution has been hard on some, and has given new life to others. It has swept away the old life so absolutely that, come what may, it will be a hundred years at least before anywhere in Russia people will be able to be unhappy in that particular way again."

The characters in Tchekov's play suffer from the lassitude that characterized the intellectuals of most western countries before the war : nor has the establishment of peace really improved their lot. Finding that their talents fail to obtain recognition in a world in which the main passport to eminence is a vulgar self-advertisement, a cultivation of the arts of popular appeal and display, at which their sensitive natures revolt, they are forced to save their self-respect by making a virtue of their impotence, which takes the form of ostentatiously renouncing the affairs of the world, and leaving them to take their own course, while they seek consolation in the realms of art and personal intrigue.

About art, they urge, there is something quintessential and sublime, which invests it with a reality which is greater than the illusory interests of the common world of men, and makes it the only object deserving the pursuit of men of intelligence. " Since the world of common men is ugly, and incidentally will have none of us, let us," they argue, " devote ourselves to the cultivation of those things of beauty which the world is so lamentably unable to appreciate." " Personal relations," they cry with Mr. E. M. Forster in " Howard's End," " are the real life for ever and ever," a phrase which has become a watchword among artistic and intellectual cliques. Thus a decadence of the intelligentsia sets in with the result that the direction of society passes to other and to less worthy hands. Where the platform grows too big for the still small voice of reason, it is captured by Cleon the leather-lunged, who feeds the mob with a carefully prepared diet, and comes to power by exploiting the simpler emotions of greed, hatred and intolerance.

Thus in the later days of the Roman Empire, when Rome, who controlled the destinies of the world, was too big to be controlled herself, we find the intellectuals straining every nerve to escape the onerous duties of public service.

The one ideal of the circle of Pliny the Younger was to get the bothersome business of public administration over as soon as possible, in order that one might pass into literary retirement, cultivate the society of one's friends and edit the poets. As the years passed and the Empire grew more unwieldy, the process of devitalization proceeded apace. The complexity of the organization and the inability to exert effective control presently produced such a deadening of interest among those who should have been the governing classes, that it was necessary to compel people to hold public office under payment of a heavy fine. The contrast with the public spirit exhibited by a small community like Athens is too obvious to require emphasis.

The difficulty of preserving the feeling that one counts in a society of such dimensions is not only the factor which contributes to the dearth of political interest: where the society is sufficiently large the political impulse is denied even that minimum of satisfaction which comes from the feeling of adequate representation, and which might otherwise have sufficed to keep it alive.

In a society of ten which is directed by two of the number, elected by the remaining eight, the impulse towards governance among the eight, although not satisfied by the direct exercise of power, receives nevertheless a kind of modified expression. The eight electors possess at least the feeling that they are adequately represented by the elected, who hold authority only by their act for the purpose of pursuing their objects. In a community such as that of ancient Athens, where public affairs were decided by the vote of the assembled citizens, the feeling of his own significance was still sufficiently strong to make of politics the dominating influence in the life of the citizen. But where the society grows to the dimensions of a modern civilized state, the numbers involved make this feeling of direct representation impossible. Where the political system is based upon a territorial unit of fifty millions or more, it is probably impossible to devise a machine which secures really direct representation. It is a commonplace that members of governing bodies are elected upon unreal issues, and that the ordinary voter exercises not the power of selection, but the power of rejection of one of two or more candidates presented to him by a kind of invisible agency. It is difficult, even for a committee, except on those rare occasions when it is unanimous, to devise a measure which expresses the real will of a majority of its members: hence the invention by political philosophers of the fiction of the "General Will" to delude people into the consoling belief that the General Will must necessarily express something! But for a community of many millions of people to devise a system which gives to each member that feeling of direct representation, which involves a sense of indirect control, and which is necessary for the maintenance of the self-respect of the political impulse is a practical impossibility.

Art and Literature as a Second String

When the many sink to apathy, and the few turn to art and literature, it is perhaps not irrelevant to point out that art and literature themselves suffer in the process. Their position, which is that of a second string, is sufficiently indicated by their quality which is second class. The ages of over-blown societies in which the intellectuals turn in disgust and despair to the creation of things of beauty, have been the Silver Ages of literature, the ages of minor poetry and realist novels, of erudition and of cleverness—the ages when inspiration was lacking.

The paralysis of the impulse to politics is a paralysis which pervades the whole system and deadens whatever it touches. When men turn to art as a substitute for politics, their art becomes bad art.

We pointed out in the first chapter how pleasure eludes us if pursued directly, and occurs incidentally when we are actively engaged upon something else. The same evasiveness is characteristic of beauty. All great literature has been a by-product of some kind of propaganda, the work of men vigorously engaged in saying something else, and when the interest in the outside world that bids us change it fails, it is useless to turn for inspiration to interest in ourselves.

Shaw remarks somewhere that the secret of being happy is not to have leisure enough to wonder whether you are miserable or not. We might add that the secret of producing great literature is to be too interested in your subject to wonder whether you are producing great literature or not. An exhibition of an author's moods in the shop-window of his novel, will not compensate for the burning interest in the world at large which produces a Swift or a Molière. Where the impulses are starved, and in particular where the impulse to take hold in the world of affairs is suppressed, men's interest in the objective world of fact wanes and perishes. Inevitably they turn for consolation to the mysteries of religion, to the cult of beauty, and to the introspective contemplation of themselves.

But the process of introspection into our own idiosyncrasies and impulses, besides withdrawing us from the service of society, tends to reduce our value and interest even as objects of introspection. Men should not turn inward on themselves and the world of feeling, but outward upon the world of fact; for it is from an absorbing interest in the world around them that men draw both the inspiration that enables them to produce great art, and the joy and energy that enable them to live happy lives.

Our impulses were not made to be understood or reasoned about: they were made to be expressed in contact with the world, and the chief link that binds us to the outside world of men is the political impulse.

Effects of Thwarting of Impulse on Morality

(b) In the second place the size of the modern State and the consequent thwarting of the political impulse, produce an adverse effect upon the general morality of the community.

Let us assume for the moment that the ethical life does in fact consist, as so many have thought, in the observance of the accepted code of morality of the particular society into which one happens to have been born. It is not difficult to show that where the State grows so large that the sense of political significance among individuals is lost, the accepted code ceases to win acceptance, and Ethics, even in the narrowly restricted sense of the word, falls into disrepute.

It will be remembered that in Chapter II, page 38 seq., certain arguments of Professor Muirhead's were considered, which sought to show that the moral code of any particular age, instead of being a purely arbitrary collection of prohibitions, could be regarded as the objectified social conscience of the sum of the individuals in the community, and that moral codes progressed because they were the reflection of a progressive moral sense in individuals.

The notion is derived from Hegel, who held that, just as the form of Government could be regarded as the concrete expression of the sum of the different wills of the individuals in a community, so the moral sense of the community was to be found embodied in the whole system of institutions and influences that make for righteousness in the State. This system of institutions and influences was summed up by Hegel in the term *Sittlichkeit* or Social Ethics. It is argued therefore that in any state of society the existing moral code does deserve recognition and respect, on the ground that it really represents the moral nature of the members of the community, just as its political institutions must necessarily represent their political nature. But in a community of the size and character of the modern State we have been describing, it is neither true to say that people do as a fact observe the accepted moral code as being representative of their own ideas about right and wrong, nor is it necessarily desirable that they should.

With regard to the question of fact, it is not necessary to enlarge here upon the complete contempt and disdain for the moral standards of our parents, which animates the existing generation, although those standards still receive acceptance and endorsement as representative of the official morality of the civilized world. Volumes have been written on the " revolt from convention " of the younger generation, and the conflict between the rigid ideas of the parent and the comparative libertinage of the children, is the stock theme of the modern realist novel.

It is true indeed that every generation embodies to some extent a revolt and reaction from the ideals of its predecessor, which provoke the querulous, " I don't know what the world's coming to ! " on the part of the aged, who see their standards disregarded. Morals in all ages have presented the appearance of becoming at once looser and more complicated to those who insist on regarding them as static, and as a consequence we find the old in every age deploring each departure from the rigidity of their own standard as a subversive lapse into immorality. " When I was young, Mr. Lydgate," says old Mrs. Farebrother in

"Middlemarch," "there never was any question about right and wrong. We knew our Catechism, and that was enough: we learned our creed and our duty. Every respectable Church person had the same opinions. But now, if you speak out of the Prayer Book itself, you are liable to be contradicted." Mrs. Farebrother might well have been speaking in the twentieth century: as a fact, she was speaking in the reign of King George IV. It is probably true that for this reason each generation seems to itself to have moved further in the way of reaction from the morals of its fathers than is in fact the case.

Admitting that these considerations may bias our judgment, we may nevertheless assert, with something amounting to conviction, that there is a special difference in moral standards and values between the present generation and those that have gone before, which is too acute to be accounted for merely by the normal swing of the moral pendulum.

The crust of morality remains the same, but the spirit has changed.

If this is indeed the case the question arises, how far it is desirable that the nominal code of society should be observed, seeing that in fact it is not observed; or, in other words, how far is the existing neglect of the morality of our elders a regrettable development. It is possible to consider the question both generally in regard to Professor Muirhead's doctrine that the State morality ought to be observed because it is the State's, and more particularly with regard to the morality of the over-blown, impulse-thwarting State of the modern world.

The State's Interest in the Maintenance of Morality

(i). With regard to the general question, it should be noted that the Hegelian notion of morality as developed by Professor Muirhead and described in Chapter II, involves the duty of obedience to the existing moral notions, whether embodied vaguely in what is known as public opinion, or more concretely in the system of State laws and institutions, on the ground that they represent the consensus of the moral instincts of the citizens. This standard of public opinion, this system of laws and institutions form together the highest expression of the morality of the time: in them the individual finds " the objective side of the organic system of impulses and desires that constitute his inward nature." The system of laws and institutions, which are the repositories of the moral standard, comes to the individual " as a species of objectified conscience. It supplies him with an objective expression of the chief content of the ideal which he himself, as sharing the intelligence and conscience embodied in these forms, is called upon to make actual." Thus it presents him with a standard whereby to correct his own instinctive moral judgments, and to which he should endeavour to make his personal conduct and notions of morality approximate. The moral order applies somewhat differently to each, owing to the differences of station and duties that exist for different individuals; but in accordance with these differences of station, the moral duties and conduct of each individual should be set in relation to the general standard.

Stripping this doctrine of the somewhat difficult Hegelian language in which it is enshrined, we may assert that, on this view, the laws and institutions of the State, together with the public opinion which they mould, may be regarded as setting the standard of morality which each individual should endeavour to observe, and that he will only stray outside them at the risk of betraying the highest which is in him. They are in fact the reflection of the highest which is in him.

Need for Changes in the Moral Code

This doctrine appears to me to cut at the basis of the possibility of moral progress. Progress in morals has always arisen from the insight and penetration of a few individuals. These individuals have invariably thrown out a rigorous challenge to the accepted morality of the State, which has done its best to suppress them. Every step in morals is in fact made by challenging the validity of the existing conception of perfect propriety of conduct. Heterodoxy in morals is regarded as scoundrelism, and what is worse, propagandist scoundrelism, which if successful will undermine society and bring us back to barbarism after a period of decadence like that which caused the ruin of Babylon, of Nineveh and of Rome.

Thus where the insight and vision of religious teachers and reformers have disclosed to men new conceptions of right and wrong and good and bad, every effort is made to arrest the development of the new standards by using the force of the State to suppress all departures from those habits of the majority which it pretentiously calls its morals.

Every moral reformer from Socrates to Christ, and from Christ to Tolstoy, has been ruthlessly persecuted by the State, and by the majority, for refusing to acknowledge the accepted code of his age, and insisting that it must be changed in accordance with the higher conception of morality which he had to announce to the world. Yet it is to such as these that moral progress is due. The fact that such men are usually posthumously ennobled, the world tumbling over itself to do them honour after it has murdered them, shows not that improvements in morality are welcomed and accepted, but that they sometimes succeed by sheer force of merit in getting themselves established at least in name, in spite of the inevitable opposition both of the State and of public opinion.

If the Hegelian theory were correct the opposition of the State in such cases would be justified on the ground that it was never possible for individuals rightly to refuse to make their conduct and moral judgments approximate to the laws and institutions of their time, or rightly to question instead of respecting that " objectified conscience " of the citizens, which is the outward expression of all that is highest in their inward selves.

It is because of this opposition that moral progress is always slow, slower than the changes in conditions and circumstances which imperatively demand it. It is slow because the proletariat, who, after strenuously resisting any attempt at change, becomes the self-appointed guardian and preserver of each innovation, so soon as it gets itself accepted, changes slowly if at all. There is probably little difference between the crowds of ancient Babylon and modern Shoreditch : hence their peculiar monopoly, the observance and retention of existing moral traditions, varies but little and slowly. It is possible in a few sentences to sum up nearly all the modifications of morality that have occurred during the whole of recorded history. A modern vice, such as mendacity, was accounted a virtue by the greatest nation of antiquity. A modern virtue, that of forgiving one's enemies, was accounted a vice proper to slaves. Drunkenness, stigmatized by ancients and moderns alike, became the mark of gentle breeding in the intermediate period. There are a few changes such as these, and what besides?

The ordinary man does not contribute anything to morality. He accepts his moral standards ready-made, just as he accepts his boots, his bacon or any other commodity. He accepts them because by acceptance he saves time and trouble. "The professional thinker," says Mr. Shaw, "may on occasion make his own morality and philosophy, as the cobbler may make his own boots: but the ordinary man of business must buy at the shop so to speak, and put up with what he finds on sale there, because he can neither make a morality for himself nor do without one."

And it is because the change and progress in morality that comes from the vision or thought of exceptional individuals, involves the trouble and labour of readjusting one's moral values, that it is always violently opposed by the conservative instinct of society as a whole, which prefers to be able to count on the expected thing being done to taking the trouble to inquire whether the right thing is being done.

As a result the needs and conditions of society change more rapidly than the moral ideas of society; the divorce laws continue to enshrine the official morality of a community which has long since passed beyond them; and most men continue to accept outworn moral codes, like the Ten Commandments, which are ridiculously out of touch with the circumstances of their time, instead of putting up with the trouble and bother which would be caused by taking a Christ seriously.

Thus it comes about that the system of laws and institutions, which are at once the prop and the mirror of public opinion, instead of being the expression of our highest selves to which we should endeavour to make our conduct approximate, are more truly the petrified husk of the living morality of a past age. Instead of making society better than its best unit, they make it worse than its average unit, because they are never up-to-date.

The truth is that a community, instead of reverently respecting the institutions and ethics it inherits from its parents as the embodiments of the wisdom of the ages, requires to change its morals as often as it changes its clothes, changes of morals being demanded by changes of circumstances, almost as frequently as changes of clothing are required by the changing seasons.

Experiments in morality should therefore be welcomed on the ground that they may point the way to a newer and better conception of the good life, instead of being reprobated because they set aside the current system of the time. It pays in fact to let such experiments take their course, although it is impossible to tell at the outset whether they will involve retrogression or progress. It pays because there is always the chance that they may involve progress, and it is only through such experiments, which are at the same time necessarily departures, that progress can come.

We may assert generally, then, that the Hegelian doctrine of Social Ethics is wrong, inasmuch as by insisting on respect for existing institutions and moral standards as such, it fails to make adequate provision for change and progress in the morality of society. It is only where the existing code is challenged that progress becomes possible.

Morality as an Ally of the Existing Order

(ii) How does this conclusion affect our consideration of the special case of the over-blown, modern society?

It will be remembered that our discussion of Hegelian Ethics arose out of the statement made above (p. 149), that one of the results of the suppression of the political impulse in the modern over-blown society is that Ethics itself falls into disrepute.

This result arises in the following way.

Although the majority of individuals in a modern society continue to identify morality with the observance of the currently accepted code, embodying the tradition of the community and supported by the authority of the State, there has arisen in modern societies a class who fiercely denounce the whole of the existing system of society, including the code of Ethics which it maintains.

Finding that society offers no scope for their political

impulse, is too big for their guidance and control, and sets no store by their capacity, they roundly demand the abolition of the whole structure of society as it exists at present, and stigmatize its codes of Ethics as a device on the part of the ruling classes for the maintenance of the *status quo*.

Reference has already been made in Chapter II to the arguments by which this school of thinkers, which is not by any means confined to extreme political theorists or to industrial revolutionaries, seeks to discredit what it calls State-manufactured Ethics. If the State is properly to be regarded, as Marx regarded it, as " an organization of the exploiting class for the maintenance of the conditions of exploitation that suited it," it is sufficiently clear that the existing code of Ethics, which is the best guarantee of the maintenance of law and order, and so of the power and security of the State, is not only conservatively obstructive to moral experiment and progress, but definitely immoral in the sense that it helps to maintain an immoral system of society. Marx's indictment of the State has been enthusiastically developed by Syndicalists and Anarchists, who, in demanding its abolition, contemplate with equanimity the ruin of the system of bourgeois Ethics which maintains it and which it helps to maintain.

Without entering into a discussion of the merits of these extreme political views, it is important to notice their adverse reaction upon current morality, and to point out that it is from the over-developed and over-complex nature of the modern State that they derive their strength.

Socialist Attack on State Morality

It is impossible to avoid observing how persistently modern Socialist literature, which is in the main thoroughly antagonistic to the State, bases its indictment of existing States upon the charge that they embody and express what Mr. Russell calls the possessive as opposed to the creative impulses. To an extreme Socialist of the type we are considering the State represents a capitalist institution, designed and controlled by a number of rich men, for the purpose of guaranteeing to them the fruits of their enterprise. In the strength and size of the modern State the possessive impulse of the rich man finds a perfect instrument for guaranteeing its own permanent satisfaction; the strength of the State in the shape of the police force providing immunity from the possessive impulses of others which he terms predatory, while its size throws a cloak of concealment over the control which he exercises in the background, and renders the work of purification and reform doubly difficult owing to the complexity of the machine.

The Socialist who takes this view of the modern State, whether from the urge of thwarted possessive impulses of his own, or from the prompting of that form of the creative impulse which I have termed the political impulse, is not likely to view with respect the code of Ethics which it sanctions and which supports it. He will see in this code a device for putting the poor man in prison for stealing on a small scale, and for conferring a knighthood on the big business man for stealing on a large scale. He will observe that not only Ethics but religion is deliberately used by the rich for the purpose of keeping the poor in their place, and deliberately flouted by the rich for the purpose of maintaining themselves in theirs.

Mr. Shaw points out that, just as the distribution of coal and blankets is undertaken by the rich in times of acute want with the object of taking the revolutionary edge off poverty, so doctrines of hope, cheerfulness, submission, and meekness, the leading doctrines of Christian Ethics, are inculcated by the rich with the object of making the poor their more willing, obedient and economical servants, the whole process being rounded off by the bribe of unlimited and inexpensive happiness in the next world, as a reward for doing one's duty in one's proper station of life in this.

This attitude to Christian Ethics is tellingly brought out in his play, " Major Barbara," where the rich capitalist, Undershaft, gives the game away by disclosing the value to his class of religion and ethical propaganda among the poor, which he rates so highly that he regards it as worth his while to buy and maintain religious organizations such as the Salvation Army simply in order that they may continue the good work.

The following quotation serves to illustrate the point:

" *Cusins*. Do I understand you to imply that you can buy Barbara ?

Undershaft. No, but I can buy the Salvation Army.

C. Quite impossible.

U. You shall see. All religious organizations exist by selling themselves to the rich.

C. Not the Army; that is the Church of the poor.

U. All the more reason for buying it.

C. I don't think you quite know what the Army does for the poor.

U. Oh, yes, I do. It draws their teeth: that is enough for me—as a man of business——

C. Nonsense! It makes them sober——

U. I prefer sober workmen. The profits are larger.

C. —honest——

U. Honest workmen are the most economical——

C. Attached to their homes——

U. So much the better. They will put up with anything sooner than change their job.

C. —happy——

U. An invaluable safeguard against revolution.

C. —unselfish——

U. Indifferent to their own interests, which suits me exactly.

C. —with their thoughts on heavenly things——

U. And not on Trade Unionism or Socialism. Excellent!

C. You really are an infernal old rascal."

That passages of this kind are not merely the exaggerated fantasies of a dramatist, but do in fact rest upon a historical foundation, there is no lack of evidence. From the days of the Industrial Revolution onwards efforts on the part of the working-classes to improve their condition have frequently been opposed on ethical grounds. The guardians of the current code of morals have sought to show that a menace to the morality of society was involved in the material betterment of the lowest classes, and have invoked the system of ethical values approved by the State and Church to discredit attempts to secure higher wages.

One instance quoted from J. L. and B. Hammond's book, "The Skilled Labourer, 1760–1832," must suffice to illustrate a tendency which goes far to discredit the ethics of State and Church with advanced political thinkers. Early in the nineteenth century the framework knitters did " a little bit of good for themselves," to the extent of earning 14s. or 15s. a week for a twelve to thirteen-hour day. A clergyman at Southwell expressed his indignation at this incident as follows: " Abundance thus rapidly acquired by those who were ignorant of its proper application has hastened the progress of luxury and licentiousness, and the lower orders were almost universally corrupted by a profusion and depravity scarcely to be credited by those who are strangers to our district."

Comment on this extract is superfluous; but it is not to be expected that those who, on whatever ground, seek to change or to modify the existing system of society will feel any respect for a code of Ethics which, as they believe, is used to thwart their efforts and to maintain the *status quo*. Those who repudiate the State on moral grounds are not likely to accept the State's morals: and the current morality of the community instead of being the objectified expression of what is highest in the conscience of individuals, comes to be regarded as an affront to their moral sense, and an impediment to the realization of their ideals.

The fact that a current system of Ethics ceases to secure respect would not in itself be a matter for regret, having regard to that need, referred to above, for a community to change its moral values in accordance with changes in its needs and circumstances. What is peculiar in the position of Ethics in the vast political organizations of the modern world, is that those whose superior vision might have prompted them to offer to the world a substitute for the morals the community has outgrown, are rendered impotent by the size of the State, and have no outlet through which to make their vision actual.

In the modern world the proper outlet for the ethical reformer is through politics; but where the political impulse is thwarted, a feeling of impotent despair ensues. The man whose vision and insight might have been of service to the world abandons the task of influencing the affairs of men in disgust and turns to the realization of some mystical Nirvana for his soul, instead of endeavouring to achieve a practical Utopia for his fellows. The aim of such men is to forget their impotence and shame by believing that the world, like themselves, is an illusion, and that true happiness is to be sought in the life within instead of in the world without. " We do not exist, we do not exist," cry the characters in Tchekov's plays.

But it is not in some mystical idealism that pronounces the world an illusion that true happiness and freedom are to be found, but in the liberation of the political impulse, and the recovery by men of the feeling that they count in the affairs of the community. Men must be made to feel again that they matter, and then they will cease to bother their heads about ethics, happiness, art, or any other substitute for the life of outward effort and achievement.

Summary of Preceding Argument

It will be desirable to summarize in a few words the argument of this section.

1. One of the most important of the impulses which are at present unduly suppressed, and for whose expression it is desirable to find an outlet, is the political impulse.

This may further be described as the impulse which prompts us to take an interest in the welfare of others and to improve their condition. Politics is the natural sphere for the expression of this impulse, since politics alone takes account of the good of the community as a whole.

2. The modern State has grown so large and its machinery of Government so complex, that the individual finds himself helpless to control its workings or to influence its decisions.

His political impulse is thwarted by the impersonality of the State, and the feeling that he counts in the affairs of society is lost.

3. This produces a devitalizing effect upon society as a whole, while the individual turns for a substitute for political activity to social work, to cynicism, to satire, or to the production of beauty for its own sake. His political impulse is driven underground and his brains are lost to the State.

4. Incidentally this produces an adverse effect upon art, the production of great literature tending to elude those who aim only at producing great literature.

5. Equally adverse is the effect upon the currently observed code of Ethics.

(*a*) In this connection, however, it is not necessarily desirable, as the Hegelian philosophers would have us believe, that the current standard should always be respected as the outward expression of what is highest in the individual. Such a theory would lead to the suppression of all departures from the existing code on the part of the individual, whereas such departures are to be welcomed as bringing with them the possibility of ethical advance. They are desirable as substituting a new code of Ethics for the existing one, which has usually been outgrown long before it is changed.

(*b*) In the modern impersonal State, however, the existing code falls into disrepute and is suspected, not by those who have a higher vision to offer to the world, but by those who see in it a device for maintaining institutions which they regard as bad. Whilst they are impotent, owing to the size of the State, to realize their own ideals, they are yet sufficiently powerful to induce others to neglect and to despise a code which they refuse to observe themselves.

If the political impulse could find expression, men would be able to create new institutions to replace those which have been outgrown, and through them to create a respect for the newer conception of morality which these institutions would embody.

The Creative Impulse in Work

IV. We have still to consider the bearing of politics upon the creative impulse as it is expressed, or rather not expressed, in the sphere of work.

Much has recently been written on the psychology of work. As opposed to the older school of thinkers, who tended to regard the normal man as an invariably lazy animal only to be spurred to effort by the prospect of monetary gain if he worked, and of starvation if he did not, there is a growing body of opinion in favour of regarding man as a being who is only able to attain happiness through continual effort, and who is bored to the point of suicide by lack of employment. Psychology of the first kind is used as the basis for the belief in the incentive provided by private enterprise and competition, as the only method of getting the work of the world done, while the second view of human nature is adopted by Socialists, Anarchists, and others who believe that the incentive of social service and the innate pleasantness of work provide a sufficient guarantee that people will perform the work that is necessary. These latter thinkers insist that the erroneous impression that man is lazy, is created not because he has any fundamental aversion to work, but because he gets too much of it, because it is too monotonous, and because it is performed under wrong conditions. A normal child has a natural desire for chocolate cakes: feed him with chocolate cakes at every meal and his innate liking will give place to violent aversion, sufficient to lead superficial critics to believe that a child is by nature a simple feeder.

We find Prince Kropotkin writing in a similar vein about work: "Overwork is repulsive to human nature, not work. . . . Work, labour is a psychological necessity, a necessity of spending accumulated bodily energy, a necessity which is health and life itself. If so many branches of useful work are done involuntarily now, it is merely because they mean overwork, or they are improperly organized." Kropotkin used this view of human psychology to justify his argument that in an Anarchist State the necessary work of the world would be willingly performed, on a basis of four hours a day all round, the unpleasant work being divided, or paid more highly either in cash or in public esteem.

As to whether this is so or not I do not pretend to hazard an opinion; but there is, I think, no doubt that to most men work is a necessity of life, which could in many cases be transformed into an outlet for what I have described in the last chapter as the creative impulse. A cursory inspection of the lives of people who are sufficiently well off to be emancipated from the business of earning a living, provides numberless examples of the necessity under which they find themselves of having to invent work which they do for nothing as a substitute for the work which other people are paid to do. Persons who are economically independent either work themselves to the bone over a hobby such as gardening or poultry farming, or adopt pursuits such as exploration or rock climbing, which will require them to do the most disagreeable and dangerous things in order to give their lives a purpose and themselves an appetite for dinner.

Human restlessness must find an outlet, and the one

which affords the most permanent satisfaction is that which issues in creative work. Most men are in fact so constituted that they find happiness and freedom not in giving rein to their passions and gratifying the whim of the moment, but in losing themselves in something outside themselves and greater than themselves, which demands unsparing effort and subordination of self to a dominant purpose.

This dominant purpose could be, but is not at present found in work. It is a commonplace, upon which it is unnecessary to enlarge, that the industrial revolution has substituted for creative work a series of highly specialized processes the performance of which requires the monotonous repetition of certain actions, varying so little that they become mechanical. In a factory, as in a business house, there is no sense either of completion or of achievement. One man does not begin one thing, continue it, mature it, and see it through to the end. He plays a small part, unendingly the same, in the production of an infinite number of the same kind of things, of none of which does he see either the beginning or the end.

To a certain extent the demands of large-scale production, coupled with the increasing use of machinery, have rendered this result inevitable; nor is it possible to restore the conditions of the Middle Ages under which the craftsman, sitting in his own workshop, performed all the different processes necessary for the manufacture of the finished article. But it may still be possible to restore something of the creative element to work, by giving to the workman the control of the condition under which he works.

To a fortunate few, to artists and to some writers, there still remains this sense of freedom in work, which enables them to invest their labours with something of the joy of creation. They work as they like, how they like, and where they like. They may, within limits, take their work away to some beautiful place and perform it when the spirit moves them. They may, if they are great enough to be able to dictate to the public taste instead of servile enough to pander to it, put of themselves what they will into their work, instead of what they think the public will like. They are not tied to any definite place, nor are they compelled to work within fixed hours: in short they control their conditions. Work is for such as these, and can be made for more, a dominant purpose in life, providing expression for man's eternal impulse to create what is new, and through creation to impose his personality upon the outside world, instead of being, as it is now, a slab of blank hours compulsorily subtracted by economic necessity from the time during which a man may live, an interruption in the business of living only to be rendered tolerable by a self-obliteration on the part of the individual, who must aim to model himself in the likeness of the machine which it is his business to serve.

How the conditions of work can be changed so that it may express instead of thwarting impulse is a problem of industry. How industry can be modified so that more provision can be made for the needs of those who work in it, is principally a problem of politics.

But it is the business of Ethics to point out that the needs of the good life as we have tried to describe it, and in particular the need to provide fuller expression for the life of impulse, urgently require such a change. The needs of the good life require such a change in order that the devitalizing process which is directly due to the overgrowth of the modern State, may be arrested in society by the liberation of the political impulse, and in industry by the liberation of the creative impulse.

Summary of Relation between Ethics and Politics

In the preceding pages I have considered the relations between Politics and Ethics from four points of view.

I dealt first with the function of politics in providing the necessary background of order and security, without which the ethical life, however we conceive of it, is impossible. This function would appear to be adequately performed by the State to-day.

In the second place I assumed the validity of that interpretation of at least some part of the good life, which I endeavoured in the last chapter to identify with the greater liberation of the creative impulses, and sought to establish the necessary function of politics in so moulding our institutions, that they provided greater scope for the expression of impulses than is on the whole the case at present.

In the third place I treated of the specifically political impulse, of its importance in the good life, and of the desirability of making greater provision for its expression in the political and social structure, which is at present too large and too complex to afford scope for the impulses and aspirations of the individual.

In the fourth place I considered the important outlet for the creative impulse which is to be found in work, and endeavoured to establish the right which Ethics has to demand from Politics that it should so mould the conditions of work, that they provide adequate expression, so far as is compatible with the needs of machine production, for the requirements of the individual.

In all these ways empirical Ethics seems to me to be intimately connected with Politics. When taking to pieces the machinery of the individual to find out what was in fact desired, we came to the conclusion that one of the most important things which is desired, but not as a rule obtained, is the liberation of the instinctive or impulsive side of human personality. But it is only through politics that such a liberation of impulse, if it is in fact desirable, can be achieved; for the conditions of our lives, which make for the expression or suppression of impulse, are largely determined by the nature of the community in which we live. If it is a problem of Ethics to determine the place and importance of impulse, it is a problem of Politics to give it scope.

I hope I shall not be thought to be trespassing too far beyond the preserves of Ethics if I consider, in the next few pages, whether political theory has as yet made any overtures to impulse, and how far such overtures take the form of proposals which would provide for the need which has hitherto been so neglected.

§ 3. New Conception of State required by Theory of Impulse

I have tried to show in the preceding pages that the suppression both of the political impulse and of the creative impulse in work arises inevitably from the size and complexity of the modern State. It is not because of any special wickedness on the part of the Government, it is not because the stage of democracy which has been reached is incomplete or is already too advanced, that the impulses of the individual fail to find expression in public and industrial life, but because the State has grown so large that what actually happens is not so much due to the will of any individual, or group of individuals, as to the interplay of forces which nullify the attempts of human will to express itself in controlling them. Treated then from the standpoint of the particular ethical theory from which we have approached politics, the function of politics may be regarded as the provision of means for the expression of human will and impulse, and the problem of politics the problem of how to make actual the will and impulses of the community.

Hitherto the view has usually been taken in political theory that only in the State is the will of the community made actual, and that it is in the State, and in no other form of organization but the State, that this will can find expression.

Reasons for this view, which finds its chief supporters in Germany where it was fully developed by Hegel, were briefly given in Chapter IV as an illustration of the methods of *a priori* reasoning. For our present purpose it is sufficient to note that in order that the theory of the State as representative of the will of the community can be plausibly maintained, a philosophic fiction called the "General Will" is invented in order that the State might exercise the function of expressing it. The General Will is held to be something different from the aggregate of all the different wills of all the individuals in a community. This aggregate is known as the "Will of All" and can clearly reside only in the community. The General Will, on the other hand, is something new, which is brought into being by the fact of the wills of a number of individuals who have a common purpose coming together, and is also something over and above the sum of those wills. It resides therefore not in the community, but in something else which is also brought into being by the fact of a number of individuals coming together into society, and which, like the General Will, is something over and above the sum of those individuals: this something else is the State.

The State has come therefore to be regarded as necessarily expressing the wills and impulses, not so much of the aggregate of all the individuals in it, but of the General Will, which is created by the fact of their being such an aggregate, and is in some mystical way more really representative than a sum of unanimous wills. Also the General Will is thought of as being always right.

To the body called the State, therefore, there has usually been attributed some unique and special function, a function which could be performed by no other body, the function of necessarily representing, whatever its character, the wills of the individuals in it, and of being the sole repository of sovereignty and power in the community.

I have given elsewhere at some length reasons for rejecting this view of the nature of the State,[1] into which it is not necessary to enter here.

It is necessary, however, to point out that if the diagnosis of the reasons for the frustration of the political impulse, given above, is in any measure correct, this theory of the nature of the State will not hold. It is not true that the State from its very nature necessarily represents the wills of everybody in it,—although some States may in fact do so— if other States, namely those modern States which both in size and complexity have outgrown the possibility of adequate control, stifle the natural outlet of the political impulse to a marked extent. We may also point out that if the State, whenever it acts, must necessarily take action which expresses the will of the community, the question naturally arises whence this controversy about the limits and scope of State action?

The conception of the State to which we have referred is in short another of the products of *a priori* reasoning, which lamentably fails to fit the facts about States as we know them. For these, and a variety of other reasons, there is a growing tendency among political thinkers to regard the State merely as a rather special piece of machinery, the political machinery of Government, and not as a unique form of human organization. This view immediately suggests the reflection that if the State is only a piece of machinery, other kinds of machinery might conceivably be designed, which would work at least as efficiently and would provide greater scope for the direct representation of individual will and the direct expression of individual

[1] "Essays in Common-Sense Philosophy," Chapter VI.

impulse. It is clear that if we conceive the main obstacle to the expression of the political impulse to lie in the size of the State, a process of devolution and decentralization, with federation of the decentralized units, will be a move in the right direction ; for where the unit of Government is small, as in the case of the Greek City State, it is easier for the individual to feel that his will and impulses can find expression.

Assuming that there is no special magic about the piece of machinery called the State, such that no other form of organization could carry out the same functions, the problem with which political thinkers are increasingly engaged, is how to devise a machinery which will perform the same functions as the national State in each of a number of small units, wherein the sense of political self-respect may be restored to the individual.

Proposals of Guild Socialists

With this end in view a number of interesting experiments have recently been made in political theory, which, whether or no they would prove practicable, would at least assist in the all-important work of liberating the political impulse, and restoring the sense of political significance. One of these experiments, the experiment known as Guild Socialism, started life as an industrial theory, concerned primarily with problems of the organization of industry, and has only recently, in the hands of writers like G. D. H. Cole, entered the field of political theory. One of its aims, and indeed the aim which it originally chiefly set before itself, was the restoration of the creative impulse in work, and it will be therefore most convenient for our purpose to examine briefly some of its proposals, since in so doing we shall be dealing with a theory which, if practicable, would achieve the double object which we formulated for politics earlier in the chapter, the object both of liberating the political impulse and providing in industry an outlet for the creative impulse.

In giving a brief outline of these proposals, our object will be not so much to consider whether they are practicable or not, a question which belongs more properly to the domain of political and economic theory, but, bearing in mind the ethical standpoint from which we are approaching the subject, to judge whether, supposing that they were practicable, they would or would not achieve that liberation of impulse which we believe to be a desirable end.

The proposals of the Guild Socialist occupy a kind of intermediate position between those of the State Socialist and the Syndicalist. The former considers the individual only in his capacity as consumer, the latter in his capacity of producer. "Both are open to the same criticism," says the Guild Socialist. "You cannot reconcile two points of view merely by denying one of them." Now the State has usually been considered to be the chief organization of the consumer, as being representative of all those people who live in a particular territorial area. It has also been regarded as the repository of sovereignty in the community. But if the individual in his aspect of producer is not to be subordinated to the individual in his aspect of consumer, it is clear that this sovereignty must be divided; and it will be divided between the State on the one hand, and the Guild Congress, a representative body of all the producers organized in their different Guilds, on the other.

The Guild Socialist therefore encourages an elaborate system of checks and balances to preserve and maintain this division of sovereignty; and, what is of the greatest significance for our own particular angle of approach, he encourages them not only in the interests of efficiency, but of individual freedom. "If," says Mr. Cole, "the individual is not to be a mere pigmy in the hands of a colossal social organism, there must be such a division of social powers, as will preserve individual freedom, by balancing one social organism so nicely against another, that the individual may still count. If the individual is not to be merely an insignificant part of a society in which his personality is absorbed, society must be divided in such a way as to make the individual the link between its autonomous but interdependent parts."

In advocating this principle of a division of sovereignty as an indispensable requisite for the restoration to the individual of a sense of freedom and independence, the Guild Socialist bases his claim upon a somewhat peculiar view of the nature of the State. In contradistinction to the Hegelian theory briefly outlined above, he regards the State simply as one among a number of associations for common purposes, primarily territorial in character. It is further defined as " the political machinery of Government in the community " (Mr. Cole, " Self-Government in Industry," Chapter V).

An important distinction is therefore made between three separate entities which are frequently confused, the State, Society, and the Community. It is clear that there are many other forms of associations of individuals for common purposes besides the State. There are, for instance, Labour bodies, churches, colleges, business companies, and all manner of voluntary associations of individuals for ethical and economic purposes, which instead of being composed, as the State is composed, of all the individuals living in a particular territorial unit, cut right across the boundaries of the nation State, sometimes falling entirely within them, sometimes including members of a number of different States. The whole complex of these associations, including the particular association called the State, is termed Society. The State is the governmental machine in Society: and that sum total of all individuals in a particular territorial unit, which stands behind and maintains both the State and Society, is called the Community. The Community is the only repository of what philosophers have called the General Will, and this General Will is not therefore vested either in the State or in any other of the associations which go to form Society; for it is only an association which represents all the purposes, which mankind has in common, which can properly be regarded as expressing and representing the General Will, and no one association of this character exists, or could exist.

What then is the nature of the particular kind of common purposes which the organization called the State exists to represent? The answer to this question can be most clearly discerned if we consider the functions and character of a local authority or municipality, which is in miniature an organization of essentially the same character as the State.

A municipality is an organization representative of all the people resident in a given locality, which is marked out by its nature for the expression of those particular purposes which they have in common by reason of the fact that they live in the same neighbourhood. It is therefore equally representative of all the persons in the locality by virtue of the fact that they are neighbours; and it represents those purposes which they have in common in connection with the provision and administration of public utilities and amenities for that neighbourhood. Its business lies therefore with public tramways and parks, with public health and housing, with public lectures and entertainments, with the public supply of gas and water, and with a variety of things which affect in an equal degree every one in the locality, and it represents people in so far, and only in so far, as they are interested in and affected by these common things. It represents them, that is, not as Protestants or Catholics, bakers or railwaymen, merchants or labourers, but as dwellers together in the same neighbourhood. It is argued that the State is in essence an organization of this kind; primarily territorial in basis, it represents people only in so far as they have interests and purposes in common, in virtue of the fact that they dwell together in the same territorial unit. It is not fitted to represent them in so far as they have purposes in common, arising from differences of creed or vocation, and does not in point of fact do so.

Having defined and delimited the essential functions which the State must perform, the Guild Socialist proceeds to consider in what way it may best perform them, and, bearing in mind the importance of restoring the sense of political self-respect to the individual, which has been lost through the over-development and centralization of the modern State, goes in for a process of wholesale devolution.

In considering this view it must be remembered that theories of this type have already worked out a scheme of devolution on a similar scale in industry. The workers are to be organized in Guilds which will control the conditions under which work is done, and will be autonomous in the sphere of production, just as the State is autonomous in the political sphere. Factories will be controlled by workshop committees and local Guilds elected by the workers, and these workshop committees and local Guilds will be represented on a National Guild body, which will be a Federation of all the local Guilds engaged in the production of a particular commodity such as cotton goods, or upon a particular kind of service, as for instance the railways. By giving to the National Guilds complete control of all matters appertaining to the conduct of industry, it is hoped to restore to those actually engaged in industry the sense of freedom and importance that comes from the knowledge that they are working directly for the community under self-imposed conditions.

The various National Guilds will themselves be federated in a Guild Congress, which will exercise in relation to industry the same kind of authority and functions as that which to-day is wielded by Parliament in the community as a whole.

Recent developments of Guild Socialism have applied to the machinery of the State a process of devolution similar to that already worked out in industry. Just as the structure of National Guilds in industry starting from the bottom, bases itself upon the workshop committee in the local factory, so the structure of the State is based upon the municipal authority which is the governing body in each of a number of local territorial units.

Starting with the notion of the State as a neighbourhood association expressing a limited number of common purposes, the Guild Socialist proceeds to ask what those common purposes are in any particular territorial unit.

The purposes which dwellers in a particular region, province or city, have in common in virtue of their " neighbourhood " relation to each other may be divided into three or four main groups. In pursuance of his principle of functional organization, that is, the principle of committing the management of certain things to persons who have special knowledge and a special qualification for the work in question, the Guild Socialist envisages the establishment of a special local or regional committee to deal with each group of purposes in each locality. In the introduction to the 1919 edition of " Self-Government in Industry," Mr. Cole groups the various functions for the performance of which local committees will be required on the following lines.

In the first place there will be required a local body of consumers, to represent and safeguard consumers' interests in relation to the Guilds of small-scale producers, tailors, bakers, butchers, and so forth, and to the Distributive Guild, in which the workers who distribute these products will be organized. The nucleus of such a body is to be found in the existing Co-operative Movement. Composed largely of housewives, it will represent the consumers' point of view in the given area in relation to these services.

Secondly there will be a local body which will deal with public amenities and the necessary provision for the mental needs of the citizens. It will be responsible for education, public lectures, parks, literature, theatres, museums, and so forth. Such functions will clearly be most adequately performed by persons differently qualified from those who will sit on a third body, which will deal with public utilities, the provision of gas, water, and light, restaurants and trams.

A fourth body will probably be necessary to administer questions of health and housing, and will again consist of persons with some expert knowledge of these matters. The necessity for each of these bodies for the purposes of Government in each local unit is defended on the Guild Socialist principle that, instead of expecting that public business will be most efficiently transacted by one body of all-round amateurs who will deal with local matters falling under each of these heads, we must consent to divide functions and to constitute special bodies of specially qualified people to perform the different classes of functions that result from the division.

It will be clear from what has been said above with regard to the Guild Socialist theory of the State, that, having started with the local authority as the primary unit of Government, we can now proceed to regard the State for most practical purposes as simply a federation of local authorities. Just as the Guild organization of industry and the professions encourages the federation of local Guilds or workshop committees into National Guilds upon which the various local Guilds will be represented, and in which they will be united, so the work of co-ordinating and unifying for the country as a whole the various neighbourhood associations, which have been outlined above, will be entrusted to national bodies composed of elected delegates from each of the associations.

Four new bodies are thus brought into existence; a National Co-operative Congress, a National Congress of

Public Education and Amenities, a National Congress of Public Utilities, and a National Congress of Public Health. These Congresses will co-operate with the appropriate National Guilds in settling national questions in regard to which the interests of producer and consumer may diverge. Possessing equal authority with the National Guilds of producers, they will, with the Guilds, be autonomous in their respective spheres.

The functions considered up to the present are those which arise directly out of the performance of services, the provision of amenities, or the production of commodities; and most of the local and national organizations of consumers which have been described will be directly related to one or more Guilds of producers.

There are, however, a number of functions in the State which fall outside this classification. Such are questions of finance, methods of taxation, the police and judicial systems and the administration and regulation of questions of personal relationship. All these questions at present fall within the sphere of the same national body, which also deals with the industrial and other services to which we have now allocated special Guild and neighbourhood associations. Proceeding upon the principle of vocational qualification for the performance of special functions adopted in the other cases, we shall now require a new local set of bodies, federated in a national body, to deal with these miscellaneous questions.

One further body remains to be described, and our outline is complete. It may be that some questions which arise between two National Guilds, or as is more likely between a National Congress of consumers and a National Guild of producers, will be incapable of adjustment. It will be necessary therefore to refer such questions to a final body or court of appeal, representative both of the National Guilds Congress and of the various Consumers' Congresses, and possessed of executive powers. Here, if anywhere, will be the final repository of such sovereignty as is left in the State. But this final court will not be in a position to initiate measures: it will only be empowered to decide such questions as are referred to it.

Provision for Impulse in Guild Socialist Proposals

I have given this brief outline of the organization of society on devolutionist lines proposed by Guild Socialists, not because I desire either to express agreement or disagreement with it, but because it will serve to illustrate the kind of results which must necessarily be worked out by political theory, if adequate expression is to be found for the ethical life, with which I have identified in part the liberation of impulse. The outline should therefore be read as an Appendix to this chapter which is primarily concerned to define the nature of the relationship between Politics and Ethics, and in particular to emphasize the importance for Ethics of the political impulse.

I do not think, however, that we are in possession of sufficient evidence to hazard an opinion as to whether the organization of society, which would be involved by the adoption of such a plan, would be practicable, and it is obvious that much remains to be done in the way of amplifying questions which are only briefly treated, and of working out details which are not even mentioned.

The significance of this experiment in political theory lies in the fact that starting from the conception of the State as a purely administrative machine,—a conception which, as opposed to the Hegelian view, is, I am convinced, a sounder one—it proceeds to apply to the business of administration which the machine performs, a process of wholesale devolution, which would in all probability have the effect both of liberating the political impulse in individuals and of restoring to the individual the sense that he counts in society. The importance of these results I have tried to show in this chapter; and I have tried in doing so to point out how their attainment is inevitably precluded to-day by the colossal size and complexity of the modern State.

The result of the process of devolution which we have outlined has been to establish in theory no less than ten different kinds of administrative bodies, upon every one of which the individual may serve, of which five, those namely which will be set up in regional areas for the transaction of public business of a local character, will be easily accessible to every inhabitant of the region. There would furthermore be nothing to prevent any individual from obtaining a seat upon one or more than one of these bodies, and once elected, he would during his period of office have ample scope and opportunity for that influence and control over the lives of his fellows to which the political impulse specifically prompts him.

To-day, he possesses in theory the same right of securing election to the one great executive body, but he is prevented from making his right effectual in practice by the strength of the forces against him, the fierceness of the competition involved and the prohibitive economic conditions attaching to the business of getting elected : while even if he secures election, the vast impersonality of the State precludes the exercise of that influence over his fellows and that sense of significance in society which the political impulse seeks to attain.

By multiplying the number of controlling and administrative bodies, by rendering them accessible to the individual, and by reducing to manageable dimensions the areas and the sphere of duties for which they would be responsible, the scheme we have been considering would at least provide scope for the political impulse, and thereby create an environment more favourable to the good life as we have conceived it.

When it is remembered that the same theory which, in the political sphere, endeavours to emancipate the individual from the obsession of the uncontrolled and impersonal State, seeks in the industrial sphere to place him in control of the conditions under which he works,—the machinery of control being again a network of workshop committees and Guild organizations not less numerous than those we have outlined in the political and administrative sphere—it becomes clear that whatever merits or demerits the theory may possess from the political and industrial point of view, and however trenchantly it may be attacked on the ground of impracticability, it would at least secure from the point of view of empirical or common-sense Ethics, an environment more favourable to the vitality of the individual through the expression of his impulses than that engendered by the modern State. It would restore the sense of individual importance in social affairs, and it would afford an opening for the creative impulse in the sphere of industry.

But this estimate of a theory which is primarily political and industrial, is only valid on the assumption that our diagnosis of the importance of impulse in the psychology of the individual,—a diagnosis which we undertook as an illustration of the method of empirical Ethics—is correct.

As this diagnosis is the basis of all our subsequent reasoning, it is perhaps desirable to inquire whether it can itself be based upon a more secure foundation than we have hitherto attempted to establish. Is there in fact any metaphysical justification for the importance which we have attributed to the purely impulsive and instinctive elements in human nature? This question I shall attempt to answer in the next chapter.

CHAPTER VII

IMPULSE AS THE EXPRESSION OF THE LIFE FORCE

§ 1. Metaphysical Basis for Theory of Impulse

I WISH in this final chapter to endeavour to relate what has been said with regard to the importance of impulse in Ethics to some sort of general view of the constitution of the Universe as a whole. In order to do this I must leave altogether the sphere of what is generally regarded as Ethics, and indulge in metaphysical speculation as to the purpose and design, if any, of the Universe, and the significance of human life and consciousness in the light of that purpose. Such speculations are not far removed from the *a priori* reasoning as to what the nature of the Universe must be, whose results in Ethics we saw reason to deplore in an earlier chapter: they require mind to pass beyond the bounds of experience, and to indulge in conjectures as to the nature of what lies behind and beyond it. But such reasoning, provided that we do not claim a dogmatic certainty for its conclusions, may not be without its uses: the criticism we passed on *a priori* speculation about Ethics was not that it was necessarily untrue to life, but that it could never be sure that it would be true to life; that, in short, it was only necessarily wrong in so far as it claimed that it must be necessarily right.

Let us admit then with regard to what follows, first that our reasoning will be in the form of conjecture and inference rather than of certain deduction from facts we have experienced, and secondly, that inasmuch as we shall be reasoning about the conditions of experience rather than about experience, conditions which, from their very nature, cannot be known, there is no guarantee of truth in any conclusions we may reach.

Although it is not possible for us to prove by *a priori* reasoning what the purpose and constitution of the Universe must be, it is the function of such reasoning to suggest fruitful hypotheses as to what it may be. Philosophy, while failing to establish the actual, enormously extends the horizon of the possible. By following its peculiar method of *a priori* reasoning on the presuppositions of our experience, it increases the breadth and scope of our speculations, setting us free from the prison of what is taken for granted, and suggesting hypotheses to act as signposts for scientific research in the realm of metaphysics, and for psychological research in the realm of Ethics.

Ethics has never been able to refrain from poaching on metaphysical preserves. It is difficult to discuss the alleged unique position of morality, or the meaning of right and wrong, without taking for granted some conception of the nature of the Universe and the business and significance of human life within it; you cannot make up your mind about the good, until you have tried to make up your mind about God.

There seem to me to be two equally important, though distinct, reasons why it is desirable to endeavour to hitch what I have said about impulse on to some theory about the Universe as a whole.

In the first place, all attempts to treat Ethics as a distinct study, apart either from religion or metaphysics, have failed. If we consider man as an isolated entity apart from the meaning and content of the rest of the Universe, we take all the stuffing out of morality, and all the driving force out of right conduct. That is why Rationalist and Secularist movements, which inculcate the pursuit of morality while denying God, have produced little else than a dull catalogue of moral affirmations, tending to the glorification of some hypostatized spirit of righteousness or an impersonal goddess of moral progress.

Progress without God has somehow meant progress without sympathy and without humour; and although we may admit that the pull of morality based on religions has mainly lain in a selfish appeal to the individual to do well for himself in the next world, at the cost of being dull on

Sunday in this one, it is nevertheless true that ethical conceptions are for the mass of men divested alike of meaning and binding force unless they are treated as the expression of some fundamental law, spirit, force, deity, call it what you will, that animates the Universe.

Thus the Secularists preach only to the elect few in little back rooms in big cities, pursuing with a sort of intensive culture a barren faith in being rational, which is divested alike of beauty and inspiration—a Rationalist hymn-book is one of the most unæsthetic things I know—whereas the religious revivalist makes converts and gets them to do good by the thousand, with the aid of an æsthetic and emotional appeal and a supernatural machinery which will not stand two minutes' rational examination. If then the Ethics of impulse is not to remain as barren as the creed of the Rationalists, it must be brought into relation with our general notion of the purpose and business of the Universe.

In the second place, I am conscious that the advocacy of the expression of impulse as I have tried to present it, looks uncommonly like another form of the pleasure philosophy discussed in the first chapter. I have tried to show that more adequate attention to the needs of impulse would mean a fuller life for the individual, and would increase the sum total of happiness and freedom. To the question why happiness and freedom are so important that they should be increased, even at considerable risk, as it might appear to some, to the observance of strict morality, no answer has been suggested up to the present, beyond the fact that happiness and freedom are pleasant, and the increase of individual pleasure is to be desired as an end in itself. But though pleasure is undoubtedly a good, I do not believe that the increase of pleasure is a sufficient foundation upon which to build an ethical doctrine. If it were, we should be committed to saying that glorified selfishness is the only incentive to morality, and that man is not capable of being swayed by considerations other than those which affect his own pleasure, a doctrine which we have already seen reason to suspect.

It is necessary therefore to seek some other support for our advocacy of impulse, a support which will derive its compelling force from something outside the narrow circle of individual pleasures and pains.

§ 2. Schopenhauer's Doctrine of the Will to Live

A convenient starting point for such a quest is supplied by the philosophy of Schopenhauer. The philosophy of Schopenhauer is not easy to follow, and his conception of Ethics is perhaps the least satisfactory part of it. The basic doctrine, however, both of his metaphysics and Ethics is one which I believe to be essentially sound.

This doctrine is that the fundamental, formative principle of the world is something which is neither rational nor conscious,—although it is the source of the activities both of reasoning and of consciousness,—which Schopenhauer called Will. By Will he meant all impulse, striving, or wanting of whatever character, and the characteristic feature of the conception, is that this Will instead of being subordinate to thought and controlled by it, is more fundamental than thought itself.

As opposed therefore to Kant, Fichte, Hegel, and the traditional line of great German philosophers, Schopenhauer held with regard to thought that instead of being the fundamental thing in the Universe, of which both the human mind and the manifold objects of sense experience, which appear to be different from mind, are modifications, thought itself was deducible from this non-rational Will or striving.

This Will expresses itself, or, to use Schopenhauer's language, is objectified in a number of different ways : these different ways are called Presentments.

The first form of Presentment is in the world of material objects with which science deals. In the second form the Will appears in the individual consciousness as the Will to live. In the third form the Will is presented in the objects of art, which Schopenhauer conceives very much in the nature of the Platonic Forms described in the third chapter. The fourth form of the Presentment of the Will is its second manifestation in the individual, as the enemy and annihilator of the Will to live, and the emancipator of the individual from the wants and strivings of the world. We are concerned here only with the second and fourth forms of the Will as Presentment.

The Will to live as manifested in the individual in the

second form of Presentment is the motive and driving force of the individual's life. It is the source of his desires, passions, instincts, impulses and reason. It is itself irrational. " The foundation and preliminary step to all knowledge of men is the conviction that the conduct of man as a whole and essentially is not guided by reason and its dictates. Hence no man becomes this or that because he has the wish to be so, however strong it may be." He does become this or that because of the Will within him, the Will which is the same Will in all of us, but differently objectified or manifested in each individual. A man's actions, thoughts, and instincts therefore, the sum total of all the mental, bodily, and emotional activities which he calls his life, are to be regarded not as the fulfilment of a moral law, or the logical deductions from some rational principle, but as the satisfaction of a prompting or urge within him of which he can give absolutely no rational account whatever. This prompting is the prompting of the Will to live, in whose service intellect and the faculties are, at any rate for most men, bound hand and foot.

The second form of the Will as Presentment is expressed therefore in the life of the normal unreflecting man. The philosopher, however, when he comes to reflect upon the operations and promptings of the Will to live, cannot but recognize that all willing implies a want, and all want implies suffering. But since the activity of the Will to live is continuous, we must not expect that the satisfaction of a particular want will lead to peace and quiescence. It will, on the contrary, be immediately succeeded by another want arising again from the promptings of the Will. Schopenhauer comes to the conclusion therefore that, from the very nature of the case, the pains of life must exceed the pleasures so long as we remain the servants of the Will.

In the philosopher, therefore, is manifested the fourth form of the Presentment of the Will, in which the Will so to speak turns against itself and endeavours to secure its own annihilation. It is only when this desirable result is accomplished and the intellect abstracted from the service of the Will, that we begin to approach the supreme good for man, which is to be found in the life of the Hindoo Yogi, who has emancipated himself from all those desires and wants tending to the continuance of life in which the Will expresses itself.

Victory over the sexual impulse, which is the expression of the Will to renew life, and over the impulse to self-preservation by the abstention from all acts calculated to preserve life, are the final stages in the victory of the Will over its second manifestation as the Will to live.

The ascetic succeeds therefore where the suicide fails; for where both are satisfied that life is not worth living, the suicide gains nothing towards the destruction of the Will, since on his death it immediately realizes itself anew in another individual, while the ascetic who destroys the Will by means of itself, cuts away the root of all consciousness. After the Will to live is destroyed, there remains no Buddhist Nirvana, no haven of rest from the conquest of the flesh and the passions, but just nothing.

The continuance of life in such a victor is of no importance, for the Will being destroyed, life becomes the mere functioning of an automatic machine. The aim and object therefore of life which is bad, is extinction which is neither bad nor good.

This brief sketch of the famous philosophy of ethical pessimism is sufficient for our purpose, in that it will serve as a guide to that principle which is to justify our philosophy of impulse. But it is not fair to abstract from this system of Ethics what happens to be of use to us, without indicating the criticisms which may validly be brought against the remainder.

Criticism of Philosophy of Pessimism

There are, I think, three reasons why, while accepting the Will-to-live principle, we may refuse to deduce from it the pessimistic conclusions which Schopenhauer draws.

(a) The first is a somewhat technical one, but cuts at the root of that renunciation of the Will to live which Schopenhauer identified with the ultimate end of Ethics in the fourth form of the Will as Presentment. It is clear that the ideal which Schopenhauer sets before himself is the ultimate extinction of human life in the Universe. This consummation is regarded as a good because the human individual, being from his very nature animated continually by the Will to live, is in consequence, for so long as he remains animated by the Will, a creature in whom pain predominates over pleasure. The extinction of want and passion with the consequent achievement of oblivion of the world is therefore regarded as a negative sort of good, since each individual who attains it administers one more rebuff to the Will to live.

But this conclusion does not follow. It does not follow because the nature of the Will, as Schopenhauer conceives it, is one and indivisible. It is the fundamental all-pervading spirit of the Universe. It appears indeed to be divisible under the forms of space and time, in which it is manifested in a number of different individuals; but this appearance is an appearance only, an appearance which belies its real nature. Hence it is not a divided part or section of it which is present in the individual: it is the whole Will, one and indivisible. "For the thing in itself, the Will to live is in every being, even the least—is present whole and undivided as completely as in all that ever were, are and will be, taken together. On this is based the fact that every being, even the least, says to himself: *Dum ego salvus sum pereat mundus.*"

But if this is the case, it is clear that the renunciation of the Will to live in any particular individual does not affect the Will in itself: there can be no question of degree in the extent to which the Will is affirmed or denied, since if it is affirmed by one only, the whole Will is nevertheless affirmed, and not only that particular section of it which would be present in a single individual, if it were possible for the Will to be divided into parts. Hence so long as one individual remains unconverted, so long as there is one who refuses to mortify his desires and renounce the Will to live, the Will to live is as completely affirmed as if all mankind continued passionately to pursue the life of need and satisfaction of need, their one recognized aim to drain the cup of desire to its dregs.

The only way, upon Schopenhauer's premises, in which the Will to live could be annihilated, would be by the single unanimous act of all conscious beings in the Universe, in whom the Will was present. Such an act might have been held out by Schopenhauer as the goal of human endeavour, had he not been precluded by his intensely individualistic

IMPULSE AS EXPRESSION OF LIFE FORCE 183

view of Ethics from contemplating as a good any act in which the individual merges his will in that of his fellows for the purposes of joint action.

Schopenhauer, therefore, while remaining entitled to recommend the attainment of self-extinction as a good to individuals, is not justified in predicating it as an absolute good for the whole human race, since the object which self extinction is designed to achieve, namely, the extinction of the Will to live itself, eludes it.

Basis of Pessimism in Egoism

(*b*) But even for individuals, the Schopenhauerian renunciation can only be considered a good if we assume a frankly hedonistic attitude to life. If we regard life as a sort of commercial speculation, success in which is only to be measured in terms of profits in pleasure over pain, then it is probably true, as Schopenhauer asserts, that life is not worth living. It is probably true because for most men pain does predominate over pleasure.

Schopenhauer's advocacy of asceticism follows directly from this estimate of the poor yield of pleasure in an ordinary life, and is based on the implied assumption that satisfaction for the individual is the only thing that matters. His asceticism is in fact only an inverted egoism. He says in effect, " Since if you live an ordinary life pursuing pleasure and avoiding pain, you are bound to get more pain than pleasure, because of the urge of the Will to live, the best thing you can do is to get rid of both pleasure and pain. It is true that by doing so you will be renouncing the possibility of pleasure, but you will be immune from the possibility of pain ; and no pleasure at all is better than a minus quantity of pleasure."

Asceticism and the renunciation of the Will is therefore only advocated on the ground that, where the individual's satisfaction is the one thing that counts, it affords the only chance of escape from a sort of business enterprise in pleasure and pain which is bound to fail.

Is Life Worth Living ?

(*c*) Not only does the Ethical ideal of asceticism implicitly assume the validity of the Utilitarian standard of pleasure as the only thing of value, a standard which we saw reason to doubt in our first chapter, but it regards the individual as an end in himself to be considered in isolation from his fellows. Schopenhauer had no use for social Ethics. An intense individualist himself, he tended to attribute disproportionate value to his own states of feeling, which he finally came to regard as so important that he was unable to conceive that others did not necessarily base their interpretation of the design of the Universe, and their estimate of its success, solely in terms of the favourable or unfavourable character of the effects it produced upon themselves. A merely introspective morality is bound in the end to regard the individual's psychological states as the only thing of supreme importance, and if what the individual finds in his own soul is not as agreeable as he could wish, he cannot avoid concluding that the Universe must be as disagreeable as himself, and condemning life as a whole because of his own lack of success in it. If the Universe is not to be condemned as a total failure, we must emancipate ourselves from the tendency to value it in terms of the individual's satisfaction or dissatisfaction with it, just as we must refuse to value that satisfaction in terms of pleasure and pain.

Apart from the technical objection which we have just mentioned, it is clear that men do not, as a whole, apply to the Universe those standards to which Schopenhauer would implicitly have us appeal. The odd thing about Schopenhauer's philosophy is that we can accept almost all his premises and refuse to draw any of his conclusions. He may demonstrate to the point of conviction that by his standards life is not worth living, and yet people, perversely enough, insist on continuing to live it. We can only conclude that where his facts are right, the rules by which he measures them must be wrong; that since by the pleasure and pain standard life is a failure, we do in fact measure success in life by something else, just as the Universe must be judged by something else.

For there is no doubt about the correctness of Schopenhauer's premises in the matter. Practically all the great poets and philosophers have concurred with him in thinking that the yield of life in pleasure does not compensate for its loss in pain. Sophocles in some famous lines concludes that the happiest lot of all is that of the man who has never been born, and that short of that, the lot most nearly happy is that of the man who, being born, quits life as soon as possible. Most of us, I believe, if asked before birth whether we would choose to live or not,—we being then assumed to be in possession of all the knowledge and experience of life that we have acquired in our present lives,—would prefer to remain unborn, on the ground that the game of life was not worth the candle. And yet if instead of presenting the question in this abstract way, we put it concretely to ourselves at this particular moment, the question namely of whether, holding the conviction we do, as to the unsatisfactory character of life considered merely as a device for the production of happiness, we would wish voluntarily to cease living now, the answer is equally in the negative. We cannot contemplate the extinction of our own personalities with equanimity, for the simple reason that the real question at issue is not whether we want life, but whether life wants us.

Existence as the Fulfilment of Definite Purpose

Here at last we get the glimpse of a new standard, which makes the Schopenhauerian assessment of life in terms of pleasure and pain unreal. If the solution of the paradox that we do not cut our losses and get rid of life, however deep our conviction of its poorness as a speculation from our own point of view, lies in the fact that life refuses to let us go, it is a solution which points on to the suggestion that life may have some purpose with us, which we are bound to carry out, a purpose for the fulfilment of which the question of our own profit in pleasure and pain is irrelevant.

If, in short, our existence is to be interpreted not in terms of our claims upon life which it is the business of life to fulfil, but of life's claims upon us which it is our business to fulfil, we have an answer at once to the paradox of why individuals persist in living although they get more misery than fun out of it, and to Schopenhauer's pessimism, which urges asceticism and the renunciation of life because life is bound to disappoint. And the answer lies simply in asserting that it is not our business to get fun out of life, but to accomplish the particular purpose of life with us which is working in us. Our question then becomes, has life a purpose, and if so, what is it?

Here we are in the region of pure speculation. It is not possible for a man to give any answer to the question propounded that will win the assent of any, except those who happen to think as he does. Questions of metaphysical truth are not capable of demonstrably irrefutable answers, which, like mathematical truths, have only to be stated to win immediate assent from all minds whatever. With regard to the proposition two plus two make four, for instance, we know not only that it is true, but that any other mind which had had no previous acquaintance with this particular proposition, would, if suddenly confronted with it, know that it was true also. It is not possible in fact for reason to think otherwise on the point.

But with regard to metaphysical questions as to the nature and constitution of the Universe, it is not possible to make any statement which may not be just as reasonably denied as asserted. It is in fact not possible either to deny or to assert purpose in the Universe with conviction, just because purpose may be both asserted and denied with plausibility.

It follows that answers to this, as to most other metaphysical questions, will depend almost entirely upon considerations of temperament, which always guide our conclusions with regard to matters which are not capable of logical proof, and often enough with regard to those which are.

The most therefore that I can hope to do is to describe very briefly certain alternative views, with regard to this question of purpose or design in the Universe, and to indicate that one of them which affords particular support to the theory of impulses already described, and brings it into relation with Schopenhauer's doctrine of the Will to live, with which I began the chapter.

§ 3. Possible Views as to Nature and Purpose of the Universe

Materialistic View of Universe

1. We may take a frankly materialistic view which denies the existence both of purpose and of spirit in the Universe. Such an outlook regards human consciousness

as a merely temporary passenger in a fundamentally hostile and alien environment, an incidental throw up that has no connection with the fundamental Reality around it. Human life has no peculiar significance, for Reality has no purpose for the fulfilment of which it can be significant; and manhood has no guarantee of permanence in the world. Not only human consciousness but life itself may be regarded as a mere eddy in the primæval slime, which happened as a fluke, and will one day ingloriously fizzle out. Such a view is only too strongly supported by the facts of geology and astronomy, tending as they do to show the insignificant part which life has played in the Universe both in point of time and of space. To quote from Mr. Wells's " Outline of History " : " Not only is space, from the point of view of life and humanity, empty, but Time is empty also. Life is like a little glow, scarcely kindled as yet, in these void immensities."

The researches of modern physics and biology corroborate geology in strengthening this conception, by showing that consciousness is an outgrowth of life which has been gradually evolved as an incidental phenomenon on a globe, originally incapable of bearing it.

On this view human life appears in an environment which is completely indifferent to it; it is a matter of mechanical adaptations and chance variations seized upon for various purposes by purely material forces, and the individual has no purpose and no object but to play out his little drama with the maximum amount of satisfaction to himself. There is no God either to reward the good or to punish the wicked, and there is no point therefore in cleaving to the straight path of duty or in refraining from the primrose path of pleasure. If the mind shrinks from the contemplation of a blank nothingness, we may, if we will, identify the vast indifference of the Universe with a sort of blind chance, which encourages human endeavours without design and thwarts them without malignity. Something of the kind is the conception which runs through most of Mr. Hardy's novels, and finds perhaps its most definite expression in the Dynasts.

The blind, mute, unseeing Thing, of which Mr. Hardy speaks, as passionless and unpitying as Fate (though even Fate might be said to have a purpose which the Thing has not), may be taken as symbolical of the nature of the Universe in which the individual finds himself; if things go well with him, it does not mean that he has deserved well; if misfortunes occur, they can be interpreted neither as punishment nor as discipline.

In a world so constituted things just happen, and it is meaningless to ask why they happen. It is typical of this attitude of Mr. Hardy's that he makes the tragedies of his novels spring logically from events which are nobody's fault, and over which nobody has any control. Thus the tragedy of the Return of the Native follows from the circumstance that when Mrs. Yeobright goes to call on her son Clym, he happens to be asleep as the result of the heat of a morning's work in the fields, and fails to hear her knock; she goes away in sorrow, and from her imagined rebuff there spring directly her own death, and more indirectly, yet equally as the result of the workings of a blind but inescapable law, the deaths of Eustacia and Wildeve.

Where human weal and woe are the result of flukes for which no one is responsible, and which none may control, there is no place for Ethics. Ethics presupposes a purpose or design which we may or may not carry out. But where there is neither God nor purpose, but only individuals chancing in an indifferent world, we can have no duties beyond our pleasures.

God as a Practical Joker

2. Sometimes, however, Mr. Hardy adopts a less non-committal attitude towards the Spirit, if any, that guides the Universe, and we have outbursts of righteous indignation against a God whose apparent object in creating mortals is to derive amusement from their vagaries under affliction. Thus there is the famous passage at the end of " Tess of the D'Urbervilles," where we are told that " Justice was done and the President of the Immortals had ended his sport with Tess."

This view finds perhaps its most vigorous expression in Goethe's Faust. Here we are asked to conceive of God as one who, becoming bored with the incessant praise and blessings of angels,—for why should they not praise him since he had done them nothing but good?—determined to create as a diversion a being called man, to afflict him with every kind of misery and evil, and yet to constitute him of so ridiculous a nature that the more he was tormented and afflicted by God, the more he would turn to Him to thank Him for his misfortunes and bless Him for his sufferings.

This view of God as the malignant practical joker, creating man, and providing him with a religious sense as a huge jest, tolerable as it is only to those in whom misfortune has developed a satirical bitterness, may nevertheless derive much evidence in its support from the phenomena of the Universe. The very incredulity with which it is received and denounced as impious by the many, would, if rightly regarded, be seen but as the subtlest part of the jest. It would be a good joke enough on the hypothesis of God's cynical malignity, for man to reject the true explanation of his sufferings as an affront to the supposed goodness of the Being who sent them. And when the cynic reads that " At San Juan in the Province of Cosoomatepec during an earthquake, the collapse of a church steeple which fell on the crowds of refugees who were praying inside the building, caused many casualties," it is difficult to convince him that his sense of perverse malignity belongs rather to himself than to God.

When we read too of the frustration of early genius in men like Keats and Barbellion, of lives such as theirs charged with fine possibilities, continuing long enough to prove their brilliance and variety, only to be suddenly extinguished, it seems to most of us such a futile trick on the part of the showman, and so strong the evidence it affords for the practical joker God, that we cannot believe that the significance of such things is just what it appears. Rather than believe that God was indeed one of whom it could be truly said " Those whom the Gods love die young," —as part of the joke, I suppose,—I for my part would prefer the view of Hardy, the view that would have us believe that circumstance has developed blindly a puppet intelligence in the midst of the Universe, which though impotent to control the strings that move it, and unable to save itself from a tragic part in the play (the beginning and end, plot and plan of which were outside its knowledge), could yet prove itself superior to all that made and compelled it, and learn to mock the blind force whose victim it was. A futile and meaningless business enough, yet better than the caustic humour of Goethe's God!

God as Omnipotent and Benevolent

3. At the other end of the scale there is the view that the Universe is the creation of a personal, benevolent and Omnipotent God. This view is immensely prevalent among the many, and has a special appeal for those who mistake the promptings of emotion for the deliverances of reason; but as an explanation of the phenomena of the Universe as we know them, there is little ground for supposing it to be true.

The belief in an Omnipotent and benevolent God derives much of its popularity from the gratifying importance that it confers upon human life. We know that our lives are immensely insignificant. We know this for a fact, and yet the knowledge is to most of us intolerable. We cannot endure that we should be of no account to anybody, and it is a natural process therefore to invent an immensely important and powerful being whose main purpose it is to watch over our welfare, and to guide and assist our footsteps. We conceive him as a terribly jealous and watchful gentleman, who carefully notes down the misdeeds of our enemies with a view to settling their account in an after life, and as carefully registers our own unrequited merit with a view to settling our account in somewhat different terms. In war time he inevitably takes the same view of the rights and wrongs of the dispute as we do ourselves, and can be relied upon in due course to see that right coincides with might.

By making our lives and welfare a matter of interest and care to a Being of such tremendous importance, we undoubtedly add to the significance of human life: and when we tack on the notion that this Being has expressly created us in his own image, even the demands of human conceit are in a fair way to being satisfied.

Under the name of theology this view has been so exhaustively discussed, criticized and defended that I do not wish to enlarge on it here; nor upon the serious logical difficulties to which it is exposed. There are, however, three observations which I should like to make, more particularly with regard to its ethical significance.

Criticism of Omnipotent God Belief
Morality as glorified Selfishness

(a) It tends to reduce Ethics, as the business of being good, to the mere necessity for pleasing some higher power in the interests of the person who is good. That this view necessarily and in all cases has this particular result I am not prepared to assert. It is, however, sufficiently clear that its practical effect upon the morality of the great mass of those who believe in it, is to make the observance of morality identical with the practice of far-sighted selfishness.

Much religion springs from the desire to lick the boots of some higher power, and apart altogether from the cruder conceptions of residence in heaven as a reward for belief and doing good, and in hell as a punishment for disbelief and doing ill, the identification of human goodness with the performance of God's will must necessarily tend to substitute as the motive for morality the desire to do God's will for the purer desire to do good as such.

It is indeed difficult on this conception to see how there can be any sanction for morality, or any incentive to the individual to be moral, except in so far as morality is pleasing to God. But the desire to be moral because it is pleasing to God cannot easily be divorced from a fairly definite conception of what the comparative effects of pleasing and displeasing God are, in so far as they touch the individual. Just as it is impossible to separate the idea of doing good from the idea of doing God's will, so it is impossible to divorce the notion of doing God's will from the effects of obedience or disobedience to the will upon oneself, with the consequent reduction of the basis of morality to the hedonistic calculus of quantity of pleasure and pain for the individual, discussed in the first chapter.

The belief in an omnipotent God can in fact have little use for Ethics. Its aim is rather to make Ethics superfluous. Where, as in the case of the religious mystic, the religious sense expresses itself in the highest and purest form of which human beings are capable, we have such a complete absorption in the oneness and goodness of God, that the petty series of trivial observances in which human morality must necessarily find its chief expression, become irrelevant to the pursuit of the good life, which is once again identified with that life of contemplation to which both Plato and Aristotle pointed the way.

This is assuredly a noble conception of the good life: but it has as little need of the specific beliefs usually associated with the view we are considering, as it has for the Ethical codes that spring from them. It is a conception that would seem to have been common to great men living in all ages, and holding all kinds of different philosophies: it does not necessarily presuppose the belief in an omnipotent benevolent God, although it has doubtless derived strength from it.

In the last resort the truth of the belief in the existence of an omnipotent and benevolent God must depend upon the nature of the religious experience of those who believe in Him. For those who possess such experience, their faith is a matter of mystical feeling and insight which, from its very privacy, is not capable of being explained to others or defended by the ordinary methods of reasoning.

Such individuals are beyond the reach of argument, not because their position is necessarily unsound, but because its truth is grasped by intuition and embraced by feeling. But just in so far as their faith remains unshaken by the assaults of rational criticism, they are unable to communicate it to others. Religious experience is like the toothache: it is an intensely private feeling which you cannot communicate to others, and of whose existence for yourself you cannot convince them. Thus the religious experience of the mystically devout is not necessarily evidence of the truth of their position, since it can have no meaning for those who are strangers to it. The words of the mystic are as words spoken to the wind, because his position depends not upon reason but upon feeling, and the truth which he would wish to convey belongs to a sphere in which argument is barren.

Thus the phenomena of religious mysticism are not only independent of ethical considerations, being an affair of private experience and not of social good, but are irrelevant to the question we are asking, namely, " Is the existence of an omnipotent, benevolent God the best explanation of the phenomena of the Universe as we know them ? " I wish to emphasize the form in which the question is put, because it forces the discussion into the region of rational controversy, in which reasoned considerations may be put forward both for and against the answer we give to it. And there is, I think, no doubt that the arguments against an affirmative answer are so strong as to be almost conclusive, if the problem is treated as a purely rational one in which feeling is not to guide our answer, except in so far as we may be unable to exclude it.

These objections may be briefly summarized under two heads, which I put forward as the second and third of the observations which I wish to make on this view.

Problem of Pain and Evil.

(*b*) Few thinkers have been able to reconcile the existence of pain and evil with the idea of a benevolent God who is at the same time Omnipotent. Volumes of controversy have been written on this subject, to which I do not wish to add anything beyond the observation that none of the numerous attempts which have been made to explain away evil and pain as illusions, due to our partial vision, or as temporary and unreal, seem to me in any way satisfactory. Even if we regard evil as due to the wickedness of man and not of God, man is himself one of God's creatures, and has the seed of wickedness implanted in him by whom ?

Nor is the presence of pain and evil confined to human affairs. Nature herself is cruel, selfish, and terribly wasteful. The young cuckoo ejects its foster brothers from the nest; some birds which lay five eggs habitually construct nests which are so small that one of the young birds is invariably squeezed out to die upon the ground. Mr. W. H. Hudson, the eminent naturalist, tells us of " slave-making ants and of the larvae of the Ichneumonidae feeding on the live tissues of the caterpillars in whose bodies they have been hatched." He describes too how wasps paralyse their prey by stinging its nerve centres, and store it in a closed cell, so that the grub to be hatched by and by shall have fresh meat to feed on,—not fresh killed meat but live meat. Instances might be multiplied indefinitely. Nature's method in its waste and cruelty has been compared to the proceedings of a man who, wishing to kill a hare, caused a field to be surrounded by sportsmen and all the guns to be let off together, or, wishing to build a house, built a whole city and abandoned all the houses to decay except one.

Waste involves pain, and pain is evil. If God is omnipotent as well as benevolent, why does He not stop it? Thus the assumption of the omnipotence of God seems inevitably to call for the conclusion as to his character described in the second view just considered.

Contradictions in the Conception.

(c) I said above that the theory of the omnipotent God was open to serious logical difficulties: " God is riddled with contradictions," says Mr. Bradley. Some philosophers have endeavoured to minimize these by making God so vaguely all-embracing as to cease to have any definable characteristics whatever. He is described as the " Eternal Witness," " Absolute Experience," " Blessed Community," " Indwelling Spirit," and so forth, each aspect, as it is called, being emphasized in turn according as it happens to be most convenient for evading the contradiction of the moment, or refuting an objection to the theory.

These contradictions may be crystallized into the question: " How out of perfect oneness and goodness can diversity and evil be generated?"

If we answer the question by saying that diversity and evil are illusory, a mere appearance which conceals an underlying unity and a fundamental goodness, our question still subsists; for the appearance of diversity and evil is as difficult to explain as the reality. From a source which is perfect unity, purely good and entirely real, it is no less impossible that error and the illusion of pain and evil should spring, than that pain and evil themselves should be generated.

And the question of motive is insoluble.

Advocates of this view tell us that pain and evil will disappear in the long run, and diversity be reconciled in a heavenly paradise, where we shall again be united with God; they explain that our time on earth is a probation, a period of training, in order that the paradise may be worthily achieved. But so it was at the beginning! Was not God always perfect?

What can be the motive of a process involving pain, error and evil by the way, of which the appointed end will be identical with the beginning? Why should what is evil ever be allowed to emerge from what is good, even if it were possible for it to do so, for the sole purpose of again being merged into it? It is impossible to conceive why such a process should ever have been begun.

Questions like these are not answered by upholders of this view; they are indeed unanswerable. The commonest form of reply is to the effect that these things are too difficult for finite human understanding, though they are doubtless plain enough to God. This reply is all very well as coming from the mystic, who definitely abrogates the claims of reason as the proper authority for dealing with such matters, and takes his stand upon his private feelings. Such a position is, as we have already remarked, unanswerable by reason, simply because it denies the validity of rational argument. But for those who endeavour to support by reason their belief in an omnipotent, benevolent God these difficulties which cannot be explained, appear to be so insurmountable as to put their theory out of court as an answer to the particular form in which we insist on putting our question, namely, " Is the existence of such a Being the best explanation of the phenomena of the Universe?" It is because of these very difficulties that the theory seems to me to fail to supply the best answer that can be given to this purely rational question, and it is presumably these same difficulties which have precluded most modern minds from holding it. It is indeed very difficult outside the Church to find any man of intelligence who really entertains this particular belief.

I turn therefore to the fourth of the views which I wish to discuss as to the ultimate purpose and constitution of the Universe.

Schopenhauer's Will as Fundamental

4. We saw that Schopenhauer's view of Ethics, a view inspired by the Will to live theory, was open to criticism on the ground that it insisted on valuing human life in terms of profits in pleasure and pain to the individual, and that it treated the individual as an isolated entity whose well-being could be considered for the purposes of Ethics apart from his relation to society. But this criticism though it is valid against the pessimism which leads to asceticism and Nirvana, does not touch the metaphysical theory of the Will to live upon which Schopenhauer based his Ethics. This theory is, I believe, correct in its postulation of some illogical, irrational principle as the fundamental thing in the Universe, as opposed to the views both of idealist philosophers, who have urged that the nature of thought, ideas or knowledge is the key to the constitution of the Universe, and of the materialists who insist that the Universe is fundamentally material.

The peculiar interest of this theory, which asserts as fundamental an irrational principle which Schopenhauer called the Will, is that it evades the difficulty which besets the frankly sceptical materialist, who puts the question " why any principle at all ? " Why, it may be asked, should we go beyond the view described under (1) above, the view that chance is the guiding principle, or lack of principle, in a Universe which is in structure fundamentally alien to human consciousness, mind and spirit, when the evidence does not warrant our doing so ?

The difficulty of this position, a difficulty to which the work of all purely sceptical writers is subject, consists in the fact that the existence of some principle in the Universe is involved in the very assertion that there is no principle. It must be some kind of use which makes us say that nothing is any use; the assertion of principle is involved in the very denial of it. Just as we cannot say there can be no knowledge, since the fact of knowledge is involved in our very statement that there is none, the knowledge, namely, that there is no knowledge, so it is that a principle of life manifests itself perforce in the very statement that there is no principle of life. We cannot deny nothing. Something must be there to enable us to deny it, and in a

IMPULSE AS EXPRESSION OF LIFE FORCE

statement such as that we are considering, it is the very principle which is denied that prompts us to make the statement.

If therefore we are to escape from a logical contradiction we must accept the fact of there being some principle, and this much being granted, I wish to call attention to the very marked tendency which has manifested itself in modern thought to identify the principle with something very like Schopenhauer's.

It will be remembered that for Schopenhauer the Will, the fundamental principle of the Universe, was a constantly active and dynamic thing, manifesting itself in individuals as the Will to Live, in the various phenomena of changing Nature and the material world, and in the objects of art. It is not rational, though it manifests itself in reason, and uses reason as the instrument whereby in the Fourth form of the objectivication of the Will as Presentment, through reflection upon the alleged inevitable conditions of life, it turns upon itself and destroys itself.

This conception of an active, changing, dynamic principle as the fundamental thing in the Universe, constantly reappears in modern thought. It appears, to mention only a few names, in the writings of Bergson, of Bernard Shaw and of H. G. Wells. Bergson calls it the *élan* vital, Shaw the Life Force, while Wells personifies it as a kind of limited but benevolent deity.

God as Personal and Limited

With Wells, indeed, this principle is elaborated in such books as " God the Invisible King," and " The Soul of a Bishop," into a militant though limited God, fighting with and for mankind against the principles of chaos and deadness and evil. We have a dualistic conception of two contradictory principles at work in the world, a conception not dissimilar from that of the Persian religion of Zoroastrianism with its good deity Ormuzd, " the spirit of wisdom and light, the very great and very good, the lord of perfection and activity, of intelligence, growth and beauty," and its evil deity Ahriman, " the spirit of darkness and malice, of crime, sin, and ugliness," who is constantly thwarting the efforts of Ormuzd to rule the world with wisdom and benevolence. Mr. Wells seems to conceive of the spirit of evil, a spirit of chaos and darkness and blankness, as somehow passively in possession of the world to begin with, and then being confronted with an active principle of good which appears, as it were, somewhat later upon the scene, and fights to rescue the world from the passively opposing dominion of the power of darkness. With this object the God of light and goodness evolves human beings to act as his allies and helpers, and looks to their brains and intelligence to carry on the struggle for him, by emancipating the world from pain, evil and error. The conception of a God who asks us to fight on his behalf, who indeed possesses no weapons for his age-long struggle, but those supplied by human will and intelligence, constitutes an inspiring appeal to mankind. It makes the conquest of pain and evil and error a conquest to be achieved by human will alone ; it provides a hope of ultimate victory ; and it sufficiently explains, what the theory of an omnipotent God cannot explain, how such things came to exist in the world. They exist not because God wills them to be there, but because they were there somehow before God, who desires through us and with our help to uproot them from the Universe.

Stimulating as this view is, I should prefer not to follow it, in so far as it personifies our principle into a limited God, with attributes akin to the human. In so doing it endeavours to make religion square with the phenomena of the Universe as revealed by science, only at the cost of affronting both religion and science. It deprives religion of its highest expression, the mystical merging of the self into something immeasurably greater and better than the self, by turning it into a sort of implied contract for business purposes where the life of mystical contemplation is tantamount to idling in office hours. It affronts the scientists by its tremendous conjectural leap beyond the evidence. Such evidence as we have is evidence for a dynamic changing force : it is only a projection of oneself that transforms it into a God. " It is," said Hobbs, " with the mysteries of religion as with wholesome pills for the sick, which swallowed whole, have the virtue to cure, but chewed are for the most part cast up again without effect." Let us therefore divest our principle or force of religious attributes, and see in what other terms we can describe it.

Conception of the Life Force

Mr. Shaw's Life Force is a principle which, like Schopenhauer's Will, expresses itself alike in human beings and in the phenomena of Nature. It is universal and all-pervading, manifesting itself in all the infinite phenomena of the Universe both mental and material. It is constantly thrusting, and pulsing, and throbbing, and it abhors the static. It is the *leitmotif*, the driving force of evolution in Nature, and of new thoughts, new emotions, new aspirations, and new impulses in man.

It proceeds by the method of trial and error, aiming always at the new, and discarding alike the old and unfit. It is this method of experiment and trial, involving the elimination of the experiments which are unsuccessful, which accounts for the appalling waste and extravagance in Nature. " Nature, we see," writes Mr. Hudson, " takes risks . . . with a very light heart : her busy brain teems with thousands, millions of inventions, and if nine hundred and ninety-nine in a thousand go wrong, she simply scraps them and goes cheerfully on with her everlasting business. An amusing person ! One can imagine some Principality or High Intelligence, a visitor from Aldebaran, let us say, looking on at these queer doings on her part and remarking : ' My dear, what a silly fool you are to waste so much energy in trying to do an impossible thing ' ! "

But the Life Force is after the same business in human beings as it is in nature. The Life Force, we must presume, has a purpose, though we may not know it. Our conception of the nature of that purpose will depend upon our temperaments. If we are what William James calls tough-minded, we shall refuse to commit ourselves by asserting it to be either good or bad : if we are tender-minded we shall believe that it is a purpose for good, which aims at the elimination of evil, pain, and deadness from the world. That such a purpose exists, however, we may be fairly certain, for all the evidence of our lives goes to show that we are brought into being for the fulfilment of purposes not our own : that in fact human beings are not ends in themselves, but means to an end outside themselves.

It is the Life Force that brings us into life, whether we like it or not. It is the Life Force which, having its purpose to achieve in the continuance of life through us, pushes us into love despite our well-meant resolutions to the contrary. And it is again the Life Force which keeps us in life, however little we may like it, until it has done with us, despite Schopenhauer's rational demonstration that life is not worth living. All the important things in life, being born, falling in love, and dying, are matters which lie entirely outside our control: in them we are the involuntary agents of something else.

As to birth it is a notorious fact, which provides an ironical commentary upon human pretensions to the rational control of life, that the most important thing about life for us, namely, whether we shall be at all, is decided for us and not by us: the only question in life about which we are never consulted is whether we shall live.

As regards love, it is true that the Life Force permits the appearance of free-will; but it is much too concerned with the production of more life for the carrying on of its own purpose to pay the slightest attention to our determination not to be guilty of the crowning folly, should we ever be foolish enough so to determine. Thus pride, honour, convenience, considerations of expediency, and even of economics, all go by the board when the Life Force impels us into activities so ridiculous, that they have made love (in others) a stock subject for comedy in all literatures in all ages.

Mr. Valentine, in Shaw's play, "You Never Can Tell," catches the right tone exactly in his speeches on falling in love: "As if Nature, after allowing us to belong to ourselves and do what we judged right and reasonable all these years, were suddenly lifting her great hand to take us, her two little children—by the scruff of our little necks—and use us, in spite of ourselves, for her own purpose, in her own way."

And as to death, it is the unfortunate tendency of people, as a whole, to fail to be either suicides or Yogis, which convicts the Ethics of Schopenhauer of the old fault of *a priori* systems, the fault of not squaring with the facts: and this failure, as hinted above, is due to the circumstance that death is not determined by the need which men may or may not have of life, but by the need which the Life Force may or may not have of them.

Proceeding as it does by the method of trial and error, the Life Force from time to time creates objects and people who, so far from carrying out its own instinctive purpose, tend to thwart and obstruct it. Obstructive objects, like people's appendices, are allowed to atrophy; obstructive people, like the Jews who crucified Christ, or the Athenians who poisoned Socrates, are corrected by the appearance of a genius among them; a genius being a specialized person who is produced by the Life Force from time to time, to give conscious expression to its own peculiar purpose. That is why geniuses are extolled after their death, and their ideas become the catchwords of the populace.

Purpose of Human Life

It will be obvious that if there is any truth in this conception, it is the business of individuals to carry forward the purposes of the Life Force. Some will do this well, some ill, and in proportion as they do it well or ill they will be happy or miserable.

It was remarked in the first chapter as a peculiarity of pleasure, that if pursued directly it eluded the pursuer, and always occurred as it were incidentally in the course of the pursuit of something else. Bringing this remark into connection with our conception of the Life Force, we may observe that it is true just in so far as it is the function of individuals not to aim at happiness for themselves, but to carry out the purpose of something outside themselves: and, if this is their function in life, it is to be expected that they should find pleasure only in the adequate performance, and miss it in the neglect of that function. The experience of mankind bears out our statement, both as to the achievement of pleasure, and as to the identification of success and happiness with the pursuit of impersonal aims. "The teaching of history," writes Mr. Wells in the "Outline of History," ". . . is strictly in accordance with the teaching of Buddha. There is, as we are seeing, no social order, no security, no peace or happiness, no righteous leadership or kingship, unless men lose themselves in something greater than themselves. The study of biological progress again reveals exactly the same process; the merging of the narrow globe of the individual experience in a wider being. To forget oneself in greater interests is to escape from a prison."

In this way it comes about that the service of the Life Force, which is chiefly expressed in devotion to impersonal ends, instead of being a slavery, offers the only avenue of escape from the narrow circle of petty wants and desires that circumscribes the self. For those who remain in that circle, the Schopenhauerian indictment of life as not worth living is valid, for they have no standard of value but that of preponderance of pleasure over pain; but for those who have gone beyond it, the standard that measures in terms of satisfaction of self is meaningless. For them life is worth living, not because of its yield in happiness, but because of its fulfilment of a purpose greater than itself.

Impulse as Expression of Life Force

What that purpose is we may not know. But if intellect and reason are given us as the instruments by which we are to pursue it, it is to the instinctive and impulse side of our natures that we must look for hints as to the direction in which we should travel.

We must regard our incurable and instinctive persistence in life and love, a persistence of which we can give absolutely no account, except that we are made like that, as a type of the more direct manifestation of the Life Force. To the promptings of all those impulses in us which seem most irrationally unaccountable, we must most of all give ear, as to the restless ever-welling surge of the Life Force within us.

Impulse is the expression of the principle of change: reason of the principle of conservation. We have already seen that all advances in social morals, originally due to the instinctive insight of the few, are caught by reason, and crystallized into a static code for the guidance of the many. This process is typical of the workings of thought, which endeavours to cast into hard and rigid forms the enthusiasm and inspiration which spring from impulse. And thought would leave it at that, unaware that the fundamental principle of the Universe is perpetual change, which will set impulse at work to break through the moulds cast by thought in morals as well as in anything else, before even they are set.

It is for this reason that the mere observance of moral codes is not a satisfactory fulfilment of the purpose of the Life Force. A moral code is a hard set thing; springing itself from impulse in the past, it refuses to give way to succeeding impulses until they break it down. Morality is petrified impulse; it is a conservation of the *status quo*, a conservation abhorrent to the Life Force, which immediately brings forth a first brood of impulses to affront it and substitute a new morality in its stead. That is why every man knows in his heart that the business of being good is not enough for the good life. That is why abstract virtue, meaning the abstention from sin and error, has become almost a term of reproach, and a man may become so worthy that people speak ill of him. The good die young it has been said, because they are so bored with the prospect of a life of being good; and indeed the Life Force has as little use for goodness as it has for happiness. It goes on its way to its own appointed goal, oblivious alike of human virtue and pleasure, caring only that human beings should become instruments adequately fitted for the ends for which it has created them.

The Life Force springs eternally in our hearts in the shape of impulse and instinct, to make us aware of the purpose it has with us, and to prompt us continually to the tasks which it would have us perform. To refuse to give ear to this prompting in the name of morals or of reason, to suppress it and to starve it is to misconceive the purpose of our lives, to renounce our function and to prove false to the principle which brought us into the world.

Summary of Metaphysical Argument

I have tried in this chapter to justify the peculiar importance attributed to impulse, by adopting a metaphysical view as to the purpose and principle of the Universe, which enables us to regard impulse as the most direct expression of that principle.

I believe that this view, though it is at best a matter of probable guessing only, is less open to objection than any of the alternative views considered in this chapter, with the single exception of that which refuses to admit that the operation of any principle in the Universe has been detected up to the present, and insists accordingly that, in the absence of evidence to the contrary, we must believe that events in the Universe have happened as the result of blind chance.

This position of complete agnosticism is admittedly little open to attack, and whether we can see fit to accept it is, I think, mainly a matter of temperament. If it is true, it reduces Ethics simply to the question of how to satisfy the individual. To answer that question we have only to find out enough about the individual, and we shall know how to satisfy him. Ethics, therefore, becomes psychology.

If, however, we adopt the Life Force view, it is clear that Ethics once again assumes the status conferred upon it by the fact of there being morality, and may invoke the necessary notion of duty as its basis. It becomes, in fact, our duty to further the objects of the Life Force as best we may; and one of the means of furthering them is undoubtedly by giving freer play to the expression of our impulses, in which the Life Force may be conceived as directly embodied.

But this principle is not the whole of Ethics. It is simply the principle at which we happen to have arrived, as the result of an experiment in the methods of what I have called empirical or common-sense Ethics. It has no pretensions to be the sum of ethical truth: it purports only to state what I believe to be a truth, arrived at by following what I regard as the only method likely to yield results which are related to life.

INDEX

Absolute, The, 91, 92, 94
Aldebaran, 199
Anarchists, 154, 159, 160
A priori theories, 89–93
Aristippus, 3
Aristotle, 7, 23, 24, 26, 103, 124, 125, 192
Athos (Mount), 38

Barbellion, 189
Beethoven, 99
Behaviourism, 105–108
Bentham, 2, 11, 13, 14, 28, 82, 116
Bergson, 197
Berkeley, 93
Bosanquet, 92
Bradley, 92, 194
Buddha, 201
Butler, Bishop, 30
Butler, Samuel, 60, 104

Categorical imperative, 25
Charity, 4
Chesterton, 48
Christ Jesus, 14, 55, 78, 122, 151, 152, 201
Church, The, 195
City State, The Greek, 36, 43
Cleon, 144
Cole, G. H. D., 166–168, 170
Commandments, The Ten, 43, 152
Comte, 43
Conscience, 29–31
Co-operative Movement, 171

Darwin, 45
Definitions, 101
Descartes, 91, 93
Desires (Unconscious), 105, 108–110
" Dynasts," 187

Economic law, 136, 137
Elan vital, 197
Elixir of Life, 59
Empiricists, 92–94
Euclid, 87
Evolution, 38–40

Factory Acts, 46, 137
Fichte, 179
Forms, 65–75, 179
Forster, E. M., 144
Freud, 95, 105

General Will, 146, 164, 165, 168
God, 69, 73, 74, 139, 177, 187, 188–195, 197, 198
Goethe, 188
Good, The, 59, 71, 74, 75, 79, 82–85
Greek City State, 36, 43
Guild Socialism, 166–175

Hamlet, 34
Hammond, J. L., and Barbara, 46, 156
Hardy, 141, 142, 187–189
" Heartbreak House," 143, 144
Hedonism, 3–10

Hegel, 89–92, 94, 132, 148–151, 153, 164, 167, 173, 179
Herodotus, 37
Hobbes, 89, 198
Hudson, W. H., 193, 199
Hume, 54, 93, 96

Imperative (Categorical), 25
Intuitionism of ends, 61–63
Introspection, 106

James, William, 93, 199
Jesus Christ, 14, 55, 78, 122, 151, 152, 201
Jung, 95, 105
Justice, 18, 19

Kant, 23–25, 26, 32, 36, 116, 132, 179
Keats, 189
Keynes, 142
Kropotkin, Prince, 160

Leibnitz, 91
Locke, 93, 96

"Major Barbara," 155, 156
Marx, 41, 154
"Middlemarch," 149
Mill, J. S., 2, 10, 12–20, 25, 79, 116, 139
Molière, 147
Moore, G. E., 62
Motive, 27–29
Mount Athos, 38
Muirhead, 38, 39, 40, 42, 147, 149

Nietzsche, 36, 48
Nirvana, 157, 181, 196

Objectivity, 51–54
"Outline of History," 187

Pater, Walter, 56
Patriotism, 4
Pessimism, 183, 196
Philosopher's Stone, 59
Plato, 65–76, 83, 84, 93, 123, 124, 179, 192

Pleasure philosophy, 3–10
Pliny, 145
Plotinus, 38
Porphyry, 83
Progress (dogma of), 42–49
Psycho-analysis, 105
Puritanism, 129

Ransome, 143
Rashdall, 6
Rationalists, 87, 178
"Return of the Native," 188
Russell, Bertrand, 46, 101, 104, 117, 119, 121, 123, 127, 154

San Juan, 189
Schopenhauer, 78, 97, 114, 179–186, 196, 197, 200, 202
Secularists, 177, 178
Self-Government in Industry, 168, 170
Sermon on the Mount, 43, 47, 79
Shaw, 130, 143, 152, 155, 197, 199
Sidgwick, 10, 33, 82
Socialism (Guild), 166–175
Socrates, 151, 201
Spencer, Herbert, 42, 47
Stoicism, 129
Subjectivity, 51–54
Suicide, 181, 200
Swedenborg, 78
Swift, 147
Syndicalists, 154, 167

Tchekov, 143
Temperance, 4
Ten Commandments, 43, 152
"Tess," 188
Tolstoy, 142, 151, 188
Tussaud, Madame, 36

Unconscious desires, 105, 108–110

Vaughan, Father Bernard, S.J., 81
Virtue, 16, 17

Wells, H. G., 187, 197, 198, 201
Whitehall, 48
Wilde, Oscar, 56, 124
Will, 125–127
Will, The General, 146, 164, 165, 168
Will of All, 164

Will to Live, 179–185, 197
Wycherly, 129

" You Never can Tell," 200

Zoroastrianism, 197

Printed in Great Britain by
Butler & Tanner
Frome and London

For Product Safety Concerns and Information please contact our EU representative GPSR@taylorandfrancis.com
Taylor & Francis Verlag GmbH, Kaufingerstraße 24, 80331 München, Germany